BARBED
ARROWS

Register This New Book

Benefits of Registering*

- ✓ FREE **replacements** of lost or damaged books

- ✓ FREE **audiobook** – *Pilgrim's Progress,* audiobook edition

- ✓ FREE information about new titles and other **freebies**

www.anekopress.com/new-book-registration

*See our website for requirements and limitations.

BARBED ARROWS

Selections That Touch the Heart,
from Spurgeon's Sermons

CHARLES H. SPURGEON

ANEKO
PRESS

We enjoy hearing from our readers. Please contact us at www.anekopress.com/questions-comments with any questions, comments, or suggestions.

Aneko Press

www.anekopress.com

Aneko Press, Life Sentence Publishing, and our logos are trademarks of

Life Sentence Publishing, Inc.
203 E. Birch Street
P.O. Box 652
Abbotsford, WI 54405

RELIGION / Christian Living / Inspirational

Paperback ISBN: 979-8-88936-228-9

eBook ISBN: 979-8-88936-229-6

10 9 8 7 6 5 4 3 2

Available where books are sold

CONTENTS

PREFACE

This volume has been compiled from the sermons of Charles H. Spurgeon. During a season of sickness and recovery, Mr. Charles Spurgeon (the son of Charles H. Spurgeon) found a pleasing pastime in organizing the illustrations, anecdotes, similes, etc., used by his beloved father in the *Discourses* published in the volumes of *The Metropolitan Tabernacle Pulpit*. Knowing how the Lord's archers desire that the arrows of truth may stick fast in the hearts of the King's enemies, it was felt that such a sheaf of arrows, so well barbed, would prove useful to brother bowmen.

The "artillery" here prepared has been proved by one of the most skillful of archers to be effective in piercing the armor joints of many sinners' harnesses, and the arrows of conviction have gone home to many hearts when shot from a bow drawn *at a venture* (1 Kings 22:34). It has been a profitable pleasure to tie up the arrows into bundles, and it is hoped that the war-worn soldiers may be relieved a little as we hand to them their ammunition in this form; for, as Charles H. Spurgeon said, "When the Word of God becomes an arrow in a man's heart, he writhes; and he would gladly tear it out; but it is a barbed shaft."

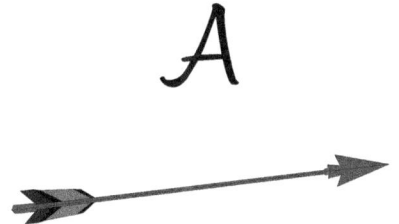

Abstinence from sin: To abstain from sin for any reason is, so far, good; yet you may abstain from sin from a motive that will lend no virtue to your abstinence. Some people abstain from sin from fear of men or from hope of gain – as the thief is honest when he sees the policeman, or as the beggar becomes pious when charity is to be obtained at church. One sin will often kill another sin, just as the miser avoids debauchery because he is too miserly to spend his money recklessly. But to abstain from sin because you love God – that is the right way and the lasting way.

Activity, useless: I heard of a Christian man whose mill wheel was seen to be in motion on a Sunday. The people going to worship wondered greatly at this. Someone who had gone by set their minds at rest by pointing out that the wheel was going idly around because the water by accident was allowed to flow over it. The man said it was like their minister and his sermons. There is no work being done, but the wheel goes around, clickety-click, clickety-click, although it is not grinding anything. This also greatly resembles many organizations for spiritual service. The water is passing over it, glittering as it flows, but the outside motion does not really meet any human need nor produce any practical result, and nothing comes of the click and hum.

Adorning the doctrine: When the famous Spartan warrior Brasidas complained that Sparta was such a small state, his mother replied to him, "My son, Sparta has fallen to your lot, and it is your duty to adorn it."

Christian, *adorn the doctrine of God our Savior in all things* (Titus 2:10). Wherever you are found, endeavor in that place to live out eternal life.

Adversity tests faith: I remember Mr. William Jay saying that birds' nests are hard to find in summertime, but anyone could find a bird's nest in winter. When all the leaves are off the trees, the nests are visible to all. Often in the days of our prosperity, we fail to find our faith; but when our adversity comes, the winter of our trial reveals the branches, and we see our faith at once. We are sure that we believe now, for we feel the effect of faith upon our character. David said, *Before I was afflicted I went astray: but now have I kept thy word* (Psalm 119:67). By keeping God's Word in the time of his affliction, he learned that his faith was really there.

Affliction, blessed: The bow of trouble shot David toward God like an arrow! It is a blessed thing when the waves of affliction wash us upon the rock of confidence in God alone, when darkness below gives us an eye to the light above.

Affliction, God's seal: Affliction is the seal of the Lord's election. I remember a story about Mr. Mack, a Baptist minister in Northamptonshire. In his youth he was a soldier, and calling on Robert Hall when his regiment marched through Leicester, that great man became interested in him and obtained his release from the ranks. When he went to preach in Glasgow, he sought out his aged mother whom he had not seen for many years. He knew his mother the moment he saw her, but the old lady did not recognize her son.

It so happened that when he was a child, his mother had accidentally wounded his wrist with a knife. To comfort him, she said, "Never mind, my bonnie boy, your mother will recognize you by that when you are a man." When Mack's mother would not believe that a sincere, fine-looking minister could be her own child, he rolled up his sleeve and said, "Mother, Mother, don't you recognize that?" In a moment they were in each other's arms. Ah, brethren, the Lord knows the spot of His children. He acknowledges them by the mark of correction.

Affliction strengthens: Your affliction strengthened your prayers. There is a man trying to write with a quill pen, but it will not make anything but a thick stroke. However, he takes a knife and cuts fiercely at the quill until it writes admirably. So we have to be cut with the sharp knife of affliction, for only then can the Lord make use of us. See how sharply gardeners trim their vines; they take off every shoot until the vine looks like a dry stick. There will be no grapes in the spring if there is not this cutting away in the autumn and winter. God strengthens and enlivens us in our afflictions through His Word.

Aimless life: Some time ago I read in a newspaper about a gentleman being brought before a judge. What was the charge against him? Nothing very serious, you will say. He was found wandering in the fields. He was asked where he was going, and he said he was not going anywhere. He was asked where he came from, and he said he did not know. They asked him where his home was, and he said he had none. They brought him before the judge for wandering. As what? A dangerous lunatic. The person who has no goal or purpose in life, but just wanders about anywhere or nowhere, acts like a dangerous lunatic, and certainly he is not morally sane.

Aimless life: Are you like a ship that is left to the mercy of the winds and waves? What a shameful condition! What a perilous case! Are you no more than a log on the water? I would not like to be a passenger on a ship that had no course marked out on the chart, no captain at the wheel, and no man at the watch. Surely you must be negligent, if not waterlogged, and you will come to a total wreck before long.

Angels, ministering: I have often admired the language of Mohammed, when in the battle of Ohod he said to his followers, pointing to their enemy, "Charge them! I can hear the wings of angels as they hasten to our help." That was a delusion on his part, for he and his men were badly beaten, but it is no delusion in the case of the servants of Christ. We can hear the wings of angels. Providence is always working with you while you are working for God.

Anger, inventive: People can always find ways of sinning against God. I remember, in my younger days, a school boy who, when at play with his companions, would fly into a furious rage and would at once throw something at the person with whom he was angry. The point I noticed was that he always had something to throw. No matter if he was in the schoolroom, on the playground, or in the street, there would always be a stone, a book, or a cup ready at his hand. So it is with those who fight against the Lord. They discover weapons everywhere in the fury of their rebellion. The evil brain is quick in devising, the depraved ear is swift in comprehending, and the sinful hand is clever in carrying out any and every scheme of disobedience to the Lord.

Answers to prayer: Yesterday I read certain notes taken by an interviewer who called on me some years ago. He reported that he said to me, "Then you have not modified your views in any way as to the efficacy of prayer?" In his description he said, "Mr. Spurgeon laughed and replied, 'Only in my faith growing far stronger and firmer than ever. It is not a matter of faith with me, but of knowledge and everyday experience. I am constantly witnessing the most unmistakable instances of answers to prayer. My whole life is made up of them.'"

Anxiety for souls: I have heard of someone brought to Christ who was a very great sinner. He had such a stiff neck that he never allowed anyone to approach him who desired his conversion. He hated the very mention of Christianity. He answered all appeals very roughly. However, one of his neighbors felt forced to go to him very early in the morning and say to him, "I beg your pardon for intruding so early, but I lay awake all last night thinking about you, and I cannot rest until I tell you something."

He answered, "What were you thinking about me for? I don't want any of your thoughts."

"Oh," said the other, "I felt so sorry to think that if you were to die, you would die without hope."

The blunt man replied, "Mind your own business."

"But," said the other man, "that is my business. I think my heart will break unless I see you saved."

The only response was, "Go away. Don't come here with any of your religious talk."

The brother went home weeping, but he was not the only one who felt his heart breaking. The blunt man went away from his forge and said to his wife, "I can always answer these religious fellows. I do not care for your pastors a bit, but that neighbor of ours has been in here, and he says it will break his heart unless I am converted; and that beats me."

He was beaten. Out of a sort of kindly pity for his neighbor's weak-mindedness, with a mixture of an unacknowledged feeling on his own account, he went to hear the preaching of the Word and was brought to Jesus.

Anxiety of soul: I remember a woman not long ago who said that while she was at her work, it came across her mind, "I am not saved." She was sweeping the room, and when she was finished, she said to herself, "I have to cook dinner, but I am not saved." She went into the kitchen and got her fire and food all ready, but the whole time she was putting things in the pot, she kept saying to herself, "I am not saved." This continued as she was busy all afternoon, and when her husband came home, she could not help blurting out, "Oh, husband, I am not saved." However, he was saved, and he pointed her to Christ. They knelt together, and oh, how he prayed with her! She found that which she so earnestly sought, and it was not many days before she could say, "Oh, husband. I am saved."

Assurance, full: A critic in an omnibus carriage said to a Christian man one day, "You have nothing to rest upon. I can prove to you that your Scriptures are not authentic."

The humble Christian man replied, "Sir, I am not an educated man, and I cannot answer your questions. However, I believe in the Lord Jesus Christ, and I have experienced such a change of character, and I feel such joy and peace through believing, that I wish you knew my Savior, too."

The answer he received was a very unexpected one. The unbeliever said, "You have got me there; I cannot answer that."

Just so, we have got them there. If we know what has been worked in us by grace, and know assuredly the sustaining power of that grace, they cannot overcome us. The person with full assurance baffles the very devil.

Assurance, occasional: Many who believe on the name of Jesus are not sure that they have eternal life; they only hope so. Occasionally they have assurance, but the joy is not abiding. They are like a minister I have heard of who said he felt assured of his salvation "except when the wind was in the east." It is a miserable thing to be so subject to circumstances as many are. What is true when the wind is in the soft south or the reviving west is equally true when the wind is neither good for man nor beast. Jesus does not want our assurance to vary with the weather or turn with the weather vane.

* * * *

- Abide after cleansing where you were before cleansing.

- A bushelful of resolutions is of small value; a single grain of practice is worth the whole.

- A cake made of memories will do for a bite now and then, but it makes poor daily bread.

- A change of life alone can prove a change of heart.

- A Christian's life should be the Ten Commandments written large.

- Additions and subtractions are weeds that are difficult to keep out of the garden of conversation.

- A defense of disobedience is a mere refuge of lies.

- Adversity has less power to harm than prosperity.

- A look of faith at Jesus breaks the heart both for sin and from sin.

- A faith that never wept is a faith that never lived.

- A frequent hearer is likely to become a fervent believer.

- A gash in the conscience may disfigure a soul forever.

- A gospel that is not for everybody is not for anybody.

- A groundless hope is a mere delusion.

- A little food cooked is better for dinner than a great roast that is raw.

- A living argument is invincible.

- All true hearts are not fit for fight.

- A man may have another heart, and yet may not have a new heart.

- Amid a torrent of sin and sorrow, you may cross the stream of time upon the stepping-stones of the places marked, *Jehovah Shammah* (*The LORD is there* – Ezekiel 48:35).

- Angels have a special liking for sleeping saints.

- An ounce of faith is better than a ton of learning.

- A pilgrim's life is not all feasting.

- A praiseful heart is a soul-winning heart.

- A quiet conscience is a little heaven.

- A rock that is in nobody's way may remain where it is.

- A saint shines on men when God has shined on him.

- As earth goes, Christ comes.

- A small musket ball at full speed will accomplish more than a large cannonball that lies still.

- A smile from Jesus in the morning will be sunshine all day long.

- A smith can shoe a horse, although he has never studied astronomy.

- A vision of God is the death of boasting.

- A week without a Sabbath is perpetual bondage.

- A wordless prayer is not silent to God.

- A working Christ makes a raging devil.

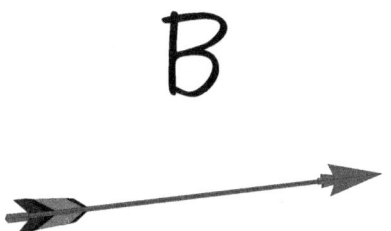

B

Believing our living: You cannot live without faith, for again and again we are told, *The just shall live by faith* (Habakkuk 2:4; Romans 1:17; Galatians 3:11; Hebrews 10:38). Believing is our living, and therefore, we need it always. If God gives you great faith, my dear brother, you must expect great trials; for in proportion as your faith grows, you will have to do more and endure more. Little boats may stay close to shore, for that is what little boats do. But if God makes you a large vessel and loads you with much freight, He intends you to know what great billows are, and you should feel their fury until you see His *wonders in the deep* (Psalm 107:24).

Believers' loyalty: Have you ever heard of the dying and wounded in Napoleon's wars who still clung to their emperor with an idolatrous love in the hour of death? Lifting himself up on his elbow, the soldier of the Old Guard gave one more cheer for the great captain. If the dying warrior saw Napoleon riding over the field, with his last gasp he would cry, "*Vive l'Empereur!*" and then expire. We read of one who, when the surgeons were trying to extract a bullet from his chest, said, "Go a little deeper, and you will find the emperor." He had him on his heart. Infinitely more commendable is the loyalty of the believer to the Lord Jesus Christ.

Bible, always right: If my compass always points to the north, I know how to use it; but if it veers to other points of the compass, and I am to judge out of my own mind whether it is right or not, I am as well off without the thing as with it. If my Bible is always right, it will lead me right; and as I believe it is so, I will follow it.

Bible, dangerous to superstition: I go into one place of worship, and I see a pretty little doll's house at the far end, and people are bowing down before some paper flowers and candlesticks. Around the building I see pictures of virgins and saints, but he who has read his Bible does not enter into the modern idolatry.

A priest once said to a poor Irishman, "No good will come of your reading the Bible."

The man replied, "It is written, *Search the Scriptures* (John 5:39). Please, your reverence, I was just reading in Deuteronomy that we should read it to our children, and the priests have no children. How can you account for that?"

"Ah!" replied the priest, "people like you cannot understand the Book."

"Well," said the man, "if I cannot understand it, it will do me no harm; and if I can understand it, it will do me great good."

That is true. The Bible is a very dangerous book to superstition, but to nothing else. Spread it, then, to the winds of heaven, and each of you read it.

Bible, inspired: This Book is inspired as no other book is inspired, and it is time that all Christians profess this conviction. I do not know whether you have read the life of our late friend, George Moore, written by Samuel Smiles, but in it we read that at a certain dinner party, a learned man remarked that it would not be easy to find a person of intelligence who believed in the inspiration of the Bible. In an instant George Moore's voice was heard across the table, saying boldly, "I do, for one." Nothing more was said. Let us not be bashful about taking the old-fashioned and unpopular side and saying directly, "I do, for one."

Bible, true: I have heard of two Roman Catholics, a man and his wife, who obtained a copy of the Scriptures. They had never seen one before. The man began to read it, and one night, as he sat beside the fire with the open book, he said, "Wife, if this book is right, we are wrong." He continued reading, and a few days after this, he said, "Wife, if this book is right, we are lost." More eager now than ever to see what the Word of the Lord was, he studied the book, until one night he joyfully exclaimed, "Wife, if this book is true, we are saved."

The same Word that showed them they were ruined also revealed the gospel of salvation. This is the glory of the Word of God; it is against us until we are led out of our sins, and then we find that death becomes the gate of life to our souls and that the Word of God is on our side. The same Word that reveals the terrors of the Lord also says, *He that believeth on the Son hath everlasting life* (John 3:36).

Blessings, opportune: God never brought you to a well and put a bucket and rope in your way without intending to fill that bucket when you let it down. When the thirsty soil has opened all its mouths to drink in the rain of heaven, that rain always comes. When the ears of wheat are ready for the sun to ripen them, the heat of harvest is near. When a man of God so looks for the Spirit that spreads the sails of hope, the breeze is sure to blow.

Blood, precious: To me there is a great sanctity about the blood of man. Last Wednesday I saw the prayer book that Bishop Juxon held in his hand as he stood by the side of Charles I on the scaffold at Whitehall. Two spots of blood are on the page of prayers that he was reading as the axe fell upon the monarch's neck. I have no reverence for Charles I, but I have reverence for drops of blood. I looked at them, and they were no matter of jest for me. The blood of a man is sacred. But what shall I say of the blood of the Son of God! God Himself, incarnate, in some mysterious manner took our humanity into union with Himself, and then shed His blood to redeem us! What is to be said of this? Look with reverence upon that precious blood.

Bookworm: I have many old books in my library in which there have been bookworms, and I have sometimes amused myself with tracing a worm. I do not know how he gets to the volume originally, but once there he eats his way into it. He bores a hole in a direct line, and sometimes I find that he dies before he gets halfway through the book. Now and then a worm has eaten his way right through from one wooden cover to another – yes, and through the cover also. This was a most successful bookworm. Few of us can eat our way quite so far. I am one of the bookworms that has not really gotten halfway into the depths of the Bible yet, but I am eating my way as fast as I can.

Burden of sin: We have seen pictures of the Arabs dragging those great Nineveh bulls for Mr. Layard, hundreds of them tugging away. I have imagined how Pharaoh's subjects, the Egyptians, must have sweated and ached when they had to drag some of the immense blocks of which his obelisks were composed, thousands of men dragging one block of masonry. I seemed to have just such a load as that behind me, and it would not budge. My burden of inward sin at fifteen years of age was such that I did not know what to do. I prayed, but it would not budge. I began reading my Bible, but my load would not move. The wheels were in deep ruts. I cried to God in my agony. I trusted Him, and the enormous weight behind me was gone.

* * * *

- Balance your duties, and do not let one squeeze another one out.

- Baptize your heart in devotion before you wade into the stream of daily care.

- Be sure the magnet is not far off when the needle is so much moved.

- Better to be Christ's patient than a Doctor of Divinity.

- Better to be in the abyss of truth than on the summit of falsehood.

- Better to face the smitings of truth than the kisses of deceit.

- Better to be God's dog than the devil's darling.

- Beware of talent in making an excuse.

- Beware of contentment with shallow grace.

- Beware of bad company in the evening!

C

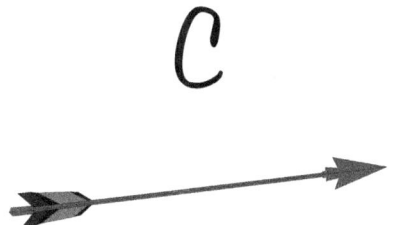

"Carry me, Father!": I am beginning to like rough places, even as Samuel Rutherford fell in love with the cross he had to carry. When the road is smooth, I have to walk; but when it is very rough, I am carried. Therefore, I feel somewhat like the little boy I saw the other night. His father had been carrying him uphill, but when he reached a piece of level road, the boy was a great lump to carry, and his father set him down and let him walk. Then the little gentleman began to pull at his father's coat, and I heard him say, "Carry me, Father! Carry me, Father! Carry me again!"

In the same way, any sensible child of God will still say, "Carry me, Father! Carry me still, I pray!" The Father's answer is, *I have made, and I will bear; even I will carry, and will deliver you* (Isaiah 46:4). Therefore, call upon Him, and ask that, when the road is rough or miry, He will carry you; and He will do so.

Caves of truth: There is a strange charm to my mind about caves. I like to visit all that are in my way. I am pleased to pass from one subterranean room to another and observe the secrets that are revealed by the glare of the torches. Here there is a spring of water, and there a grand stalactite. Here is an ascending staircase leading to another hollow, and there you must go down by a ladder to a greater depth. This is a fair allegory of the way in which the Spirit of God leads us into all truth. In God, even in Christ Jesus, *are hid all the treasures of wisdom and knowledge* (Colossians 2:3), and within these hiding places we find our habitations.

David was so much at home with God that he entered by earnest trust into one attribute after another, and he delighted in them all.

Ceaseless warfare: It is with us Christians as it was with the Highlanders in battle when their leaders called out to them, "Lads, there they are. If you don't kill them, they will kill you." There is no room for peace. It is war to the knife, not only now, but to life's end.

Charity by proxy: This is the age of proxy, or having others act for us. People are not charitable, but they beg money from somebody else to be charitable with. It is said that charity nowadays means that A finds B to be in distress, and therefore asks C to help him. Let us not avoid our duty in this way. Go and do your own work, each person bearing his own burden and not trying to pile a double load on other people's shoulders. Brethren, from morning until night, sow beside all waters with unsparing hand.

Chastisement, proof of love: Mr. Samuel Rutherford, writing to a lady who had lost five children and her husband, said to her, "Oh, how Christ must love you! He would take every bit of your heart to Himself. He would not permit you to reserve any of your soul for any earthly thing." Can we stand that test? Can we let all go for His sake?

Child of God, preciousness: How precious in the sight of the Master His saints are! I have been trying to work out a calculation: if the hairs of their heads are worth so much that God registers them, what are their heads worth? Who can tell me that? If their heads are worth so much that the Lord Jesus Christ died to redeem them, who can tell what their souls are worth, or rather what they are not worth? They are worth more than all the worlds put together. Ask a mother what her child is worth. "What will you take for your boy, ma'am?" My friends, if she sold him at the price she would consider a fair compensation, none of us could come up with the amount, even if we put all that we have into one common fund. The Lord set such a value on His children that He gave His Son Jesus Christ to die rather than that He would lose one of them, and Jesus Himself chose to die on the cross so that none of His little ones would perish. Oh, the value and the preciousness of a child of God! Worlds would not serve for dollars to be the basis of the valuation.

Children, idolized: It is very common to idolize children. A mother who had lost her baby agonized and rebelled about it. She happened to be in a meeting of the Society of Friends, and there was nothing spoken that morning except this word by one female Friend, who was moved, I do not doubt, by the Spirit of God to say, "Verily, I perceive that children are idols." She did not know the condition of that mourner's mind, but it was the right word, and she to whom God applied it knew how true it was. She submitted her rebellious will, and at once was comforted.

Stop idolizing these little men and women, for although you value them, they are of the race from which you are to cease. Stop idolizing them, for their breath is in their nostrils, and indeed it is but feebly there in childhood. A proper and right love of children should be cultivated, but to carry this beyond its due measure is to grieve the Spirit of God. If you make idols of children, you have done the worst you can for them, whether they live or die. Cease from such folly.

Christ, all in all: The first line of the covenant of grace is Jesus Christ. The last line of the covenant of grace is Jesus Christ. Everything in between is the Lord Jesus Christ. Begin with Him as A, and go right through to B, C, D, E, F, and so on until you end with Z, and it is all Jesus Christ. He is all. Yes, He is all in all.

Christ for all: I remember in Martin Luther's life that in one of the Roman Catholic churches, he saw a picture of the pope, cardinals, bishops, priests, monks, and friars all on board a ship. They were all safe, every one of them. As for the laity, poor wretches, they were struggling in the sea, and many of them were drowning. Only those were saved to whom the good men in the ship were so kind as to hand out a rope or a plank. That is not our Lord's teaching: His blood *is shed for many* (Mark 14:24), and not for the few. He is not the Christ of a caste or a class, but the Christ of all conditions of all people. His blood *is shed for many for the remission of sins* (Matthew 26:28).

Christ glorified: You will glorify Christ by mending the socks of the little ones quite as surely as by washing His feet with tears.

Christ loved best: We love relationships, but as compared with Him, we could hate father and mother and sister and brother for His name's sake (Luke 14:26). When a certain martyr was about to be burned, they brought out his wife and his eleven little children and instructed them to kneel in one long row to ask their father, for their sakes, to consent to deny the faith and live; but as he kissed them one by one, and lingered longest over the dear mother of them all, he said, "I would do anything for your sakes, my dear ones, that I might live with you, but since it is for Christ, my Lord's sake, I must tear myself away even from you." When Jesus is in the soul, the idols leave their thrones. He loves us out of the pit of idolatry.

Christ omitted: A famous picture has been recently produced that represents our Lord before Pilate. It has deservedly won great attraction. A certain excellent newspaper, which brings out a large number of engravings for a very cheap price, has given an engraving of this picture; but inasmuch as the painting was too large for the paper to give the whole picture, they have copied a portion of it. It is interesting to note that they have given us Pilate here, and Caiaphas there, but since there was no room for Jesus upon the sheet, they left out that part of the design.

When I saw the picture, I thought that it was wonderfully characteristic of a great deal of modern preaching. See Pilate here, Caiaphas there, and the Jews over there – but the Victim, bound and scourged for human sin, is omitted. In the case of the publication, it is possible that the figure of the Christ will appear in the next issue; but even if He should appear in the next sermon of our preachers of the new theology, it will be as a moral example, and not as the Substitute for the guilty, the Sin-bearer by whose death we are redeemed. When we hear a sermon with no Christ in it, we hope that He will come out next Sunday. At the same time, the preaching is, so far, spoiled, and the presentation of the gospel is entirely ruined as long as the main figure is left out.

Oh, it is a sad thing to have to stand in any house of prayer and listen to the preaching, and then have to cry out, *They have taken away my Lord, and I know not where they have laid him* (John 20:13). Rest assured that they have laid Him in a tomb. You may be quite certain of that. They have put Him away as a dead thing, and to them He is as good as dead.

True believer, you may comfort your heart with the recollection that He will rise again. He cannot be held by the bonds of death in any sense, and though His own church should bury Him and lay the huge lid of the most enormous casket of heresy upon Him, the Redeemer will rise again, and His truth with Him, and He and His Word will live and reign together forever and ever.

Christ, only foundation: Having once made Christ my foundation, I will take a page out of the book of the Puritans of Massachusetts. I have heard that in their early days, their counselors agreed "that the State of Massachusetts should be governed by God, until they had time to find a better rule." In the same way, I will rest on Christ alone until I can find a better resting place. When we find that God has laid another foundation, we will look at it. When we discover a foundation more suitable for sinners than the sinner's Savior, we will consider it – but not until then.

Christ's presence, salvation: Have you not seen people engaged in earnest work who did not understand their business? They were apprentices and other unskilled people simply throwing away time. They were making bad worse and running great risk. Perhaps a great calamity will occur if the work is not done well and quickly. A first-rate workman is sent for. A man has come who understands the business. He says, "Let me come! Move out of my way! You are on the wrong track. Let me do it myself!" You have not blamed him for egotism, for the thing needed to be done, and he could do it, while the others could not. Everybody recognized the master workman and gave place to him. The announcement of his coming was the end of the chaos and the signal of hope. Even so, Jesus comes to you sinners, and in His presence is your salvation.

Christ receiving sinners: When one of our professional beggars knocks at a door and gets well received, he is very likely to send another. I have heard that vagrants make certain marks near the door by way of telling others of their group which are good houses to call at. If you want many beggars at your house, feed one and another of them well, and birds of the same feather will flock to you. You know how one sheep leads another, and perhaps when some come to Christ, many others will follow.

Christ the way: Some time ago, a minister in America was going up the aisle of his church during a revival when a young man earnestly cried to him, "Sir, can you tell me the way to Christ?"

"No," was the answer, very deliberately given. "I cannot tell you the way to Christ."

The young man answered, "I beg your pardon. I thought you were a minister of the gospel."

"So I am," was the reply.

"How is it that you cannot tell me the way to Christ?"

"My friend," said the minister, "there is no way to Christ. He is Himself the way. All who believe in Him are justified from all things. There is no way to Christ. Christ is here."

Christ to be fed upon: What is the use of bread if it is never eaten? If you go to the orphanage, you will see a large batch of bread there kept upon the shelves. Now suppose that I were to go down there and say to the baker, "Lock that door. I want to keep that bread. I am going away for a while, and I will take the key with me so that I may save that bread." Suppose I were to do so, and would return in a couple of months' time. Should I say to myself, "I have saved that batch of bread"? I am afraid that it would turn out not to be very wise and beneficial. Let us go and look at the loaves that we have kept from use! Come away at once! The sight is not pleasant. Decay and corruption have fallen upon what we have hoarded. The bread would not be very good at all.

Why, it is the very purpose of bread, the object of bread, the portion of bread, to be eaten. It is honored in being eaten by the orphans. It would be degraded by being left to grow stale and moldy. Now the Lord Jesus Christ is never so honored a Christ as when sinners come and feed upon Him. This precious Bread must be eaten, or it has not answered its purpose.

Christ triumphant: "There," said a dying man in a ditch, when the great Emperor Napoleon rode by, and he heard a shout of victory. "Let me die. The emperor has conquered." And oh, may not you and I be well content to be blotted out and forgotten as long as Christ the King will come to His own again? He will soon triumph.

"Christ would be the loser": A Scottish minister told the story of an aged saint who, on her dying bed, said that her Savior would never leave her to perish. She was asked, "But suppose that He did not keep His promise, and you were lost?"

She answered, "He would be a greater loser than I." When asked what she meant, she answered, "It is true that I would lose my soul, but God would lose His honor and glory if He were not true."

If we have trusted in God and have come out of the Egypt of the world through His grace and have left all our sins behind us, if we were left to die in the wilderness, the Lord Jesus Christ would lose His glory as a Savior, the divine Father would lose His name for immutable faithfulness, and the Holy Spirit would lose His honor for perseverance in completing every work that He undertakes. The Lord God of Israel will never stain His glory. Therefore, be confident that He who brought you out of Egypt will bring you into Canaan.

Christians, like eagles: As I rode along in the south of France, the driver turned to me and exclaimed, "Look, there are eagles!"

"No," I said, "they are not eagles, for eagles fly alone."

Seven or eight large birds together might be hawks or falcons, but not true eagles. A royal eagle soars alone into the blue. His mate may bear him company, but he has no crew of comrades around him. The child of God, the true eagle of the skies, when he rises into the divinest and deepest ranges of his spiritual life, is and must be alone.

Christians, neglectful of means of grace: At a prayer meeting some time ago, one brother prayed that the Lord would bless those who were at home on beds of sickness and on sofas of wellness. The last words were unexpected, but very needful. Certain of our friends practice the art of staying at home, but I fear they do not divide the spoil. As to prayer meetings and weeknight lectures, they are regarded as tasks more than privileges by many professing Christians. They live on one meal a week.

Christians, "Off and on": I heard of a brother who claimed to have abstained from alcohol for a long time, but some doubted. When he was asked how long he had been an abstainer, he replied, "Off and on for twenty years." You should have seen the significant smile upon all faces. An abstainer off and on! His example did not stand for much. Certain professing Christians are Christians off and on, and nobody respects them.

Christians on duty: A policeman wears a badge to show that he is on duty, and all believers should feel that such a badge is worn upon their very heart day and night.

Christians, pilgrims: We are pilgrims. We journey along a road that has not been smoothed by a steamroller, but remains as rough and rugged as a path to an alpine summit. We push on through a wilderness where there is no way. Sometimes we traverse a dreary road comparable to burning sand. At other times sharp trials afflict us as if they cut our feet on sharp stones. Our journey is a maze, a labyrinth. The Lord leads us up and down in the wilderness, and sometimes we seem further from Canaan than ever. Seldom does our march take us through gardens. Often it leads us through deserts. We are always traveling, never staying long in one place.

Christians, so called: A boy in the streets who was selling mince pies kept yelling, "Hot mince pies!" A person bought one of them and found it quite cold. "Boy," he said, "why did you call these pies hot?"

"That's the name they go by, sir," said the boy.

In the same way, there are plenty of people who are called Christians, but they are not Christians. That's the name they go by, but all the substance is drained out of them by other matters.

Christians, some like old china: My venerated grandmother owned a set of fine china, a part of which, I believe, is still in use now. Why does it exist now? It has seen little service. It only came out on high days and holidays, maybe once in six months, when ministers and friends came to tea. It was a very nice set of old china, too good for children to break. Some Christians are like that fine old china. It would not do to use them too often. They are too good for every day.

They do not teach their employees or try to win the poor people in their neighborhood to Christ, but they talk well at a conference. Oh, you fine bits of eggshell china, I know you. Don't be afraid. I am not going to break you, yet I would somewhat trouble you by the remark that in the case of such ware as you are, more pieces get broken in the cupboard than on the table. You will last longer if you get to work for Christ in everyday work. Jesus was not sent out only for special occasions, and neither are you.

Christians, valley: Numbers of Christians seem to always live in the marshes. If you go through the valleys of Switzerland, you will find yourself becoming feverish and heavy in spirit, and you will see many people with mental and physical afflictions. However, if you climb the sides of the hills and ascend into the Alps, you will not meet with that kind of thing in the pure, fresh air. Many Christians are of the sickly valley breed. Oh, that they could get up to the high mountains and be strong!

Church, back door to the: One good old lady I know of used to say sarcastically that she hoped the church would take care that the back door was easy to open, for she was quite sure that if so many came in at the front, there would be a good number who would soon have to be thrown out at the back. I am half afraid that she hoped it would be so to justify her criticisms.

Church, dead: A dead church is a reeking Golgotha, a breeding place of evils, and a home of devils. The tombs may be newly whitewashed, but they are nonetheless open sepulchers, haunts of unclean spirits. A church all alive is a little heaven, the resort of angels, the temple of the Holy Spirit. In some of our churches, everybody seems to be a little colder than anybody else. The members are holy icicles. A general frost has paralyzed everybody, and although some are colder than others, yet all are below zero. There are no flowing streams of refreshment, but everything is bound hard and fast with the frost of indifference.

Oh, that the Lord would send forth His wind and melt the glaciers. Oh, that the Spirit of God would chase winter out of every heart and every church. No human power can keep a church from a frostbite that numbs and kills. Unless the Lord is there, growth, life, and warmth are all impossible.

Church of God, enduring: Standing in the Colosseum at Rome, as I looked around on the ruins of that vast house of sin, I could not help but praise God that the church still existed although the Colosseum is in ruins. Anyone standing there when the thousands upon thousands gloated their eyes with the sufferings of Christians would have said, "Christianity will die out, but the Colosseum, so firmly built, will stand to the end of time." But indeed, the Colosseum is a ruin, and the church of God is more firm, more strong, and more glorious than ever.

Confidence misplaced: I remember speaking with a person who was concerned about one of the great speculations that brought loss and ruin to many. As I looked into his honest face and heard his openhearted talk, I said to myself, "This is not a man who is capable of robbery or deceit. He is a plain, blunt, farmer-like sort of man who might even be a victim of the confidence trick." I later learned that this is the usual style of the man who flatters a group or betrays a trust. Of course, if a man looks like a thief, you button up your pockets and smile if he invites you to take shares, but you are not as careful when the person appears to be the embodiment of simple honesty. The woman in the carriage who picks your pocket looks like the last person to be capable of such a thing, and that is why she is able to do it.

Transfer this knowledge to other matters, and it may save you sorrow. If you start trusting anybody with a blind confidence beyond what you should give, and especially if you trust your soul with any priest or preacher, whoever he may be, you are a fool, and your folly may result in everlasting harm that can never be undone.

Contingencies, none with God: With God, there are no contingencies. The mighty charioteer of Providence has gathered up all the reins of all the horses, and He guides them all according to His infallible wisdom. There is a foreknowledge and predestination that concerns all things, from the motion of a grain of dust on the threshing floor to that of the flaming comet that blazes across the sky. Nothing can happen except what God ordains; therefore, why should we fear?

Conversion: A man may turn his head, and only turn a little; he may turn his hand without there being much movement of the whole body; but when he turns his feet, he turns himself completely. The turn we sinners all need is a whole turn.

Conversion cannot be hidden: I remember a poor man who was converted, but he was dreadfully afraid of his wife (he is not the only man in the world who is in that fear). Therefore, he was fearful that she would ridicule him if he knelt to pray. He crept upstairs in his stockings so that he might not be heard but could have a few minutes of prayer before she knew he was there. His scheme failed. His wife soon discovered what he was doing. Genuine conversion is not to be hidden any more than a candle in a dark room. You cannot hide a cough. If a man has a cough, he must cough; and if a man has grace in his heart, he will show grace in his life.

Conversion, delayed: I have heard of a man who had long attended one of the official churches in Scotland, and as he did not get any good, he went off to listen to certain irregular preaching, and there he found peace with God. The old minister warned him of his wickedness in being away from the church, and said, "Donald, you should not have gone to hear that man; he is not of the old church."

"Well," said Donald, "but I wanted a blessing, and I felt I must go anywhere to get it."

"Well, Donald," said the minister, "you should have waited at the pool, like the man in the gospels, until the water was stirred."

"Well, sir," said the man, "that man saw that the water was sometimes stirred, and although he did not get in himself, yet he knew that others stepped in and were healed, and that encouraged him to wait a little longer in the hope that his turn might yet come. But I have lain at your pool these forty years, and I never saw the water stirred, neither did anybody get healed in it, so I thought it was time for me to look somewhere else."

Indeed it was. We cannot afford to be lost for the sake of churches or chapels.

Conversion, joy in heaven: I remember Mr. Knill speaking of his own conversion. He used an expression that I would like to use concerning one of you. Here it is: "It was just a quarter past twelve, August second, when *twang* went every harp in paradise; for a sinner had repented."

Conversion, remarkable: There was someone who went to hear Mr. Whitefield. He was a member of the "Hellfire Club," and he was a desperate fellow. He stood up at the next meeting of his abominable associates, and he delivered Mr. Whitefield's sermon with wonderful accuracy, imitating his very tone and manner. In the middle of his exhortation, he himself was converted and came to a sudden pause. He sat down brokenhearted and confessed the power of the gospel. That club was dissolved. That remarkable convert was Mr. Thorpe of Bristol, whom God so greatly used afterward in the salvation of others. I would rather have you read the Bible to mock at it than to not read it at all. I would rather that you came to hear the Word of God out of hatred to it than that you never came at all.

Conversion, strange: I read a story in the *Life of John Wesley* about a group of Methodists meeting in a barn, and how certain of the villagers who were afraid to break through the door resolved to place someone inside who would open the door to them during the service so that they could disturb the congregation. This person went in before the service began, and he concealed himself in a sack in the corner of the barn. When the Methodists began to sing, he liked the tune so well that he would not get out of the sack until he had heard it through. Then followed a prayer, and during that prayer, God worked on the man in the sack, and he began to cry for mercy. The good people looked around and were astonished to find a sinner in a sack seeking his Savior. The door was not opened to the mob after all, for he who intended to do so was converted. It does not matter why the people come to hear the gospel; God can bless them in any case.

Conversion, strange: A young man had been under a sense of sin for some time, longing to find mercy, but he could not reach it. He was a telegraph clerk. One morning he was in the office and needed to receive and transmit a telegram. To his great surprise, he spelled out the words of John 1:29: *Behold the Lamb of God, which taketh away the sin of the world.* A gentleman who was on a vacation was telegraphing a message in answer to a letter from a friend who was in trouble of soul. It was meant for someone else, but he who transmitted it received eternal life as the words came flashing into his soul.

Conversion, sudden: I knew a man who had lived a life of carelessness and indifference, with occasional outbursts of drunkenness and other sins. One day this man happened to hear a preacher say that if anyone would ask anything of God, He would give it to him. The assertion was much too broad and might have done harm, but this man accepted it as a test and resolved that he would ask, and thus would see if there was a God. On the Saturday morning of that week, when he was going early to his work, the thought came upon him, "Perhaps there is a God after all." He was ready to faint as the possibility struck him, and there and then he offered the test petition concerning a matter that concerned himself and his fellow workmen.

His prayer was granted in a remarkable manner, and he came then to be a believer in God. He is more than that now, and he has found his way to be a believer in all that God has spoken. He has found peace through believing in Jesus Christ. It struck me as wonderful that this man, who never before had any concern at all for Christ, would suddenly be turned to serve the living God. That preacher never had a more unlikely hearer, yet he succeeded with him.

Conversion, sudden: There must be a moment in which the man is dead, and another moment in which he is alive. I grant you that life would be very feeble at first, but there still must be a time in which it was not there at all; and again, there must have been an instant in which it began. There can be no middle condition between dead and alive, yet a person may not know when the change took place. If you were going to the Cape, you might cross the equator at the dead of night and know nothing about it, but you would still cross it. Some poor countrymen have thought that they would see a blue line right across the waves, but the equator is not perceptible, although it is truly there. The equator is quite as real as if we could see a golden belt around the globe.

Dear friends, I want you to cross the line this morning! Oh, that you might say, "Glory, glory, hallelujah! God has had mercy upon me!" Although you feel that you would not give two cents for your life, if you come to God through Jesus Christ, you will go away blessing God not only that you are alive, but that you will live forever, happy in His love.

Conversion, surprising: The chaplain of a jail, a dear friend of mine, once told me of a surprising case of conversion in which a knowledge of the covenant of grace was the main instrument of the Holy Spirit. My friend had under his charge a man most treacherous and brutal. He was especially evil, even in comparison with other convicts. He had been renowned for his daring and for the complete absence of all feeling when committing acts of violence. I think he had been called "the king of the executioners."

The chaplain had spoken to him several times, but had not succeeded even in getting an answer. The man was perversely set against all instruction. At last he expressed a desire for a certain book, but as it was not in the library, the chaplain pointed to the Bible that had been placed in his cell and said, "Did you ever read that book?" He gave no answer, but looked at the good man as if he would kill him. The question was kindly repeated, with the assurance that he would find it well worth reading.

"Sir," said the convict, "you would not ask me such a question if you knew who I was. What have I to do with a book such as that?"

He was told that his character was well known to the chaplain, and that for this very reason he recommended the Bible as a book that would be appropriate for his situation. "It would do me no good," he said. "I am past all feeling." Doubling up his fist, he struck the iron door of the cell and said, "My heart is as hard as that iron; there is nothing in any book that will ever touch me."

"Well," said the chaplain, "you need a new heart. Did you ever read the covenant of grace?" The man answered sullenly by enquiring what he meant by such talk. His friend replied, "Listen to these words: *A new heart also will I give you, and a new spirit will I put within you"* (Ezekiel 36:26). The words struck the man with amazement, as well they might. He asked to have the passage found for him in the Bible. He read the words again and again.

When the chaplain came back to him the next day, the wild beast was tamed. "Oh, sir," he said, "I never dreamed of such a promise! I never believed it possible that God would speak in such a way as that to men. If He gives me a new heart, it will be a miracle of mercy; yet I think He is going to work that miracle upon me, for the very hope of a new nature is beginning to touch me as I was never touched before." That man became gentle in manner, obedient to authority, and childlike in spirit.

Conversion, unexpected: There was a woman who had been in such a dreadful despair that she would not even hear the gospel for years. She became very ill, and she said to one who called upon her, "You sent a man to preach under my window three months ago, and I got a blessing."

"No," the friend said, "I did not send anyone to preach under your window."

"Oh," she said, "I think you did, for he came and preached, and my maid said there was nobody listening to him. I did not want to hear him, and since he was quite loud, my maid closed the window, and I lay down in bed. However, the man shouted so that I could not help hearing him, and I thank God I did, for I heard the gospel and I found Christ. Did you not send for him?"

"No," said the good man, "I did not."

"Well," she said, "then God did. There was nobody in the street listening to him, but I heard the gospel, and I got out of my despair. I found the Savior, and am prepared to die."

Convincing testimony: I remember the story of a lawyer who attended a class meeting. He heard about a dozen people tell what the Lord had done for them. He said as he sat there, "If I had a case in court, I would like to have these good people as witnesses. I know them all. They are my neighbors. They are simpleminded people, straightforward and honest, and I know I could carry any case if I had them on my side." Then he very straightforwardly argued that what they all agreed upon was true. He believed them in other matters, and he could not doubt them in this, which was to them the most important of all. He tried Christianity for himself, and the Lord heard him. Very soon he was at the class meeting adding his witness to theirs.

If I were to ask this question to you now, what would you say? You who have had answers to prayers, say "Yes." I am sure that there are none of us who have ever tried the power of prayer who would have to say "No." If I were to ask the contrary question, who has prayed and has not had an answer to prayer, there would be no answer. All who are inclined to pray will vote with those who say "Yes."

Courage: Splendid was the courage of Alexander when they told him that there were hundreds of thousands of Persians. He said, "Yet one butcher does not fear myriads of sheep."

Another person said to him, "When the Persians draw their bows, their arrows are so numerous that they darken the sun."

"It will be fine to fight in the shade," cried the hero. Oh, friends, we know whom we have believed (2 Timothy 1:12), and we are sure of triumph!

Covenant, the: Remember the old Scottish wife who thanked God for the porridge, and then thanked Him that she had a covenant right to the porridge since He had said, *Verily thou shalt be fed* (Psalm 37:3). Oh, it makes life very sweet to take everything from the hand of a covenant God and to see in every mercy a new pledge of covenant faithfulness! It makes life happy, and it also inspires a believer to do great things for his gracious God. Standing on covenant ground, we feel consecrated to the noblest ends.

Covenanters, the: In my bedroom, I have hung up a picture of an old Covenanter. He sits in a wild glen with his Bible open before him on a huge stone. He leans on his great broadsword, and his horse stands quietly at his side. Evidently, he smells the battle afar off and is preparing for it by drinking in some mighty promise. As you look into the old man's face, you can almost hear him saying to himself, "For the crown of Christ and the Covenant, I would gladly lay down my life this day." They did lay down their lives, too, right gloriously, and Scotland owes her covenanting fathers far more than she knows.

It was a grand day when they spread the Solemn League and the Covenant upon the tombstones of the old churchyard in Edinburgh, and all sorts of men came forward to set their names to it. Glorious was that roll of worthy men. There were the lords of the Covenant and the common men of the Covenant. Some of them pricked a vein and dipped the pen into their blood so that they might write their names with the very fluid of their hearts. All over England also there were men who entered into a similar solemn league and covenant and who met together to worship God according to their light, and not according to books of human order. They were resolved upon this one thing – that Rome should not come back to place and power while they could lift a hand against her; neither should any other power in throne or Parliament prevent the free exercise of their consciences for Christ's cause and covenant.

These stern old men with their firm beliefs have gone, and what do we have in their places? Indifference and frivolity. We have no Roundheads and Puritans, but then we have scientific dressmaking, and we play lawn tennis! We have no contentions for the faith, but then our amusements occupy all our time. This wonderful century has become a child and has put away manly things. Self-contained men, men in whom is the true grit, are now few and far between as compared with the old covenanting days.

Credulity: Credulity toward man and unbelief toward God are remarkable things to find in the same person. We cannot help seeing in the daily newspapers how easily people are deceived. Get up a prospectus and a list of names as directors, including a pauper with a fancy title, and you can bring in money by wagon loads. The confidence trick can still be successfully performed. One impostor lived for months by calling at the door of simple old people in almshouses, telling them that a cousin in America had died and had left them a fortune, but it was essential for fees to be paid at the government offices, and then the inheritance would be handed over at once. Time after time, the money was scraped together, the crook went on his way, and no more was heard of the cousin in America. There are so many people around who lack good sense and good judgment that con men reap harvests all year long.

Cross – our all, the: The cross is all I need for security and joy. Truly, this bed is long enough for a man to stretch himself upon. The cross is a chariot of salvation in which we travel the high road of life without fear. The pillow of atonement heals the head that aches with anguish. I sit down with great delight beneath the shadow of the cross, and its fruit is sweet unto my taste. I have no impatience even to hurry to heaven while resting beneath the cross, for our hymn truly says:

> Here it is I find my heaven,
> While upon the cross I gaze.[1]

Cross – our sign, the: As Constantine saw the cross in his dream and took it for his emblem with the motto "By this sign I conquer," so today our only hope of victory for the gospel is that the cross of Christ displays it and the name of Jesus is in it. His name is named on us, and in His name we will cast out devils and do many mighty works until His name will be known and honored wherever the sun pursues its course or the moon cheers the watches of the night.

* * * *

- Children of shame may be made heirs of glory.
- Christ often frequents cottages.
- Christ is all blessing.
- Christ is ready for every emergency.
- Communion with God is a great maker of music.
- Constancy is the proof of sincerity.
- Continued delay of duty is a continuous sin.
- Conversion days are our high holidays.
- Conversions are not run into molds.
- Cries are not for musicians, but for mourners.

---

1   This is from a hymn by James Allen (1734-1804) that begins with "Sweet the moments, rich in blessing."

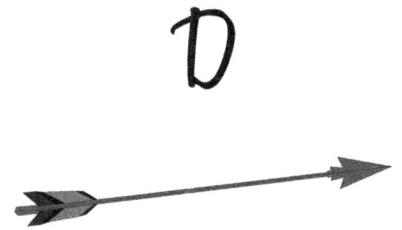

Death day: I came this week out of a quiet bedroom where I saw a Sunday school teacher passing away. It was a little sanctuary. Everything was so quiet, peaceful, and happy. Death cast no shadow over the sweet face. Heaven lit the features. It seemed more like a marriage day than a death day. Why are these dying beds so happy? Is it because these people have any goodness of their own? Far from it. Without exception, they deny it. Is it because they are strong and independent? No. I could speak of young and old believers who are greatly weakened by a long sickness, yet are as greatly strong in faith. What brings this peace? Truly, the Lord was there. His presence realized makes death a small matter. This is why we sing the hymn by Isaac Watts that says:

> Oh, if my Lord would come and meet,
>   My soul should stretch her wings in haste,
> Fly fearless through death's iron gate,
>   Nor feel the terrors as she passed.

The presence of God with the soul of a believer swallows up death in victory, and anything else that is terrible in time or in eternity loses its terror in the presence of the mighty God of Jacob.

Decision delayed, difficult: I sometimes think that God treats people as Benjamin Franklin treated the man who stood loitering in his book-shop, who at last picked up a book, and asked, "How much is this?"

Franklin replied, "A dollar."

"A dollar?" he said. "A dollar?" and he would not pay the price. After staying for about ten minutes he said, "Come, Mr. Franklin, now what will you take for it?"

Franklin answered, "Two dollars."

"No," he said, "you are joking."

"I am not joking," said Franklin. "The price is two dollars."

The man waited and sat awhile, thinking, "I want the book," he uttered. "Still, I will not give two dollars. What will you take for it?"

Franklin said, "Three dollars."

"Well," said the man, "why do you raise your price?"

Franklin responded, "You see, you have wasted so much of my time that I could better have afforded to have taken one dollar at first than three dollars now."

Sometimes if people come to Christ at the very first invitation, it is sweet and easy to come, but when people wait, when they postpone believing, when they violate conscience and tread down all the uprising of holy thoughts within them, it becomes much harder for them to trust in Christ than it would have been when He was first preached to them.

Decision, needed: If confessors, reformers, martyrs, and covenanters had been unfaithful to the name and faith of Jesus, where would the churches of today have been? Must we not be strong and courageous and bold as they were? If we are not, are we not condemning our fathers? Is it not very inspiring to read of Martin Luther and his brave deeds? Of course, everybody admires Luther! Yes, yes, but you do not want anyone else to do the same today as he did.

When you go to the zoological gardens, you all admire the bear, but how would you like a bear at home or a bear wandering loose about the streets? You tell me that it would be too much, and no doubt you are right. So we admire a man who was firm in the faith four or five hundred years ago. The past ages are a sort of bear pit or iron cage for him, but such a man today is a nuisance and must be put down. Call him a narrow-minded bigot, or give him a worse name if you can think of one.

Yet imagine if in those past ages Luther, Zwingli, Calvin, and their colleagues had said, "The world is out of order, but if we try to set it right, we will only make much trouble and get ourselves into disgrace. Let us go to our rooms, put on our sleeping clothes, and sleep through the bad times, and perhaps when we wake up things will have gotten better."

Such conduct on their part would have imposed upon us a heritage of error. Age after age would have gone down into the infernal deeps, and the destructive bogs of error would have swallowed all. These men loved the faith and the name of Jesus too well to see them trampled on. Observe what we owe them, and let us pay to our sons the debt we owe to our fathers. It is the same today as it was in the Reformers' days. Determination and fortitude are needed. This is the day for the man; where is the man for the day? We who have had the gospel passed to us by the hands of martyrs dare not trifle with it nor sit by and hear it denied by traitors who pretend to love it, but inwardly abhor every line of it. The faith I hold bears upon it marks of the blood of my ancestors.

Deliverance through trust: Years ago, the Mentonese desired to break away from the dominion of the Prince of Monaco. They therefore drove out his agent. The prince came with his army. It was not a very great one, it is true, but it was still formidable to the Mentonese. I do not know what the high and mighty princeling was going to do, but the news came that the King of Sardinia was coming up in the rear to help the Mentonese, and therefore his lordship of Monaco very prudently retired to his own rock. When a believer stands out against evil, he may be sure that the Lord of Hosts will not be far away. The enemy will hear the dash of His horse's hooves and the blast of His trumpet, and will flee before Him. Therefore, be of good courage and compel the world to say of you, *He trusted on the LORD that he would deliver him* (Psalm 22:8).

Desires: There are vast desires in us all, and when we are impassioned, those desires expand and enlarge. Man feels that he is not in his element and is not what he intended to be. He is like a bird in the shell – he feels a life within him too great to be forever confined within such narrow bounds. Do you not, dear friends, feel great longings? Does not your soul burn with high ambitions? Our immortal nature groans beneath the burden of mortality; its spiritual nature is weary of the chains of materialism. That hungering will never be hushed into contentment until we receive Christ; but when we have Him, we learn that we are the sons of God, heirs of God, *joint-heirs with Christ* (Romans 8:17), and that *it doth not yet appear what we shall be: but we know that, when he shall appear, we shall be like him; for we shall see him as he is* (1 John 3:2).

Devotion, wholehearted: The pearl fisherman standing on the rock plunges deep into the sea. He does not know whether or not he will bring up a pearl that will decorate an emperor's diadem, but he searches the deeps in that hope. Why should he not bring up such a treasure as well as anybody else? It does not matter if the fisherman himself is coarse and ragged and rugged; he may still find a priceless pearl. And you, whoever you may be, I direct you in the name of the eternal God to plunge yourself into your work with wholehearted devotion, and you will yet discover some hidden jewel that will adorn Immanuel's crown.

Differences ended: Imagine if a child would say to his father: "Father, I will not come to see you on your birthday. I will not join with the rest of the family in the usual celebration."

"Why not?"

"Because my brother is not what he should be, and until he mends his ways, I will not celebrate your birthday."

The father would say, "My dear son, is that any reason why you should not remember me? Certainly I am not to blame for what your brother does. Come to the celebration and think of me."

So I say to you that if you have any personal angers and differences, do not smother them, but end them.

Differing feelings divide: According to the well-worn fable, two people who are completely different in their pursuits cannot live well together. The person who washes clothes and the person who burns charcoal were obliged to part, for whatever the laundry worker had made white, the charcoal producer blackened with his finger. If differing pursuits divide, much more will differing feelings upon a vital point divide. It is Jesus whom Jehovah likes to honor, and if you will not trust even Jesus with your soul's salvation, you grieve the heart of God, and He can have no pleasure in you.

Difficulties: When out in a boat in the Clyde River, we came opposite the great rock called the Cock of Arran. Our captain did not steam right ahead and rush at the rock. No, for he did what was much wiser. He cast anchor for the night in the bay at the foot of it so that we were sheltered from the wind by the vast headland. I remember looking up through the darkness of the night and admiring its great sheltering wing. It began as a difficulty, but it became a shelter. Every now and then in Scripture you come before a vast truth. Will you steam against it and wreck your soul, or with better wisdom, will you cast your anchor under it?

Divinity, marrow of: When the gospel seemed to have died out in Scotland under the reign of Moderatism, one earnest man by accident came across a little book, Fisher's *Marrow of Divinity*. He was enlightened as to the pure truth of God. He began at once to preach its truth, and thousands of people rejoiced in it. That marrow has never been taken away from Scotland's bones since, nor can it, nor will it, no matter what the devil may do. A desperate and subtle attempt is now being made, but it will be certainly overcome through the wisdom of God.

Doing more: Never talk of what you have done, but move on to something else. An officer rode up to his general and said, "Sir, we have taken two guns from the enemy."

"That is good," said the general. "Take two more."

Doubt, cure for: When a soul has drawn near to Jesus and has been fed by Him, it is no more troubled with doubts than a man at the equator is bitten by frost.

"I believe in the Bible," one person said.

"How can you do that?" sneered another.

"Because I know the Author," was the good reply.

If you are walking in the light with your Lord, questions and doubts are heard no more, but you delight in deep restfulness of soul, knowing that it is the Lord.

Drones, or idle people: I wonder whether we will ever have a day such as the bees celebrate in its due season. You may, perhaps, have seen them dismissing those who are not productive. It is a remarkable sight. They say to themselves, "Here are a lot of drones eating our honey, but never making any; let us turn them out." There is a dreadful buzz, is there not? But out they go. I do not intend to turn you out, or to make a buzz, but if ever those who do work for Christ should burn with a holy indignation against those who do nothing, some of you will find the place too hot for you.

Dwarfs and giants: When we stand with dwarfs, we think we are giants, but in the presence of giants, we become dwarfs. When we think of the departed saints and remember their patience in suffering, their diligence in labor, their fervor, their self-denial, their humility, their tears, their prayers, their midnight cries, their intercession for the souls of others, and their pouring out their hearts before God for the glory of Christ, we shrink into less than nothing and find no word of boasting on our tongue. If we survey the life of the only Perfect One, our dear Lord and Master, the sight of His beauty covers our whole countenance with a blush.

Dying in the dark: A child of God may die in the dark. One person said to old Mr. Dodd, the quaint old Puritan, "How sad that our brother should have passed away in darkness! Do you doubt his safety?"

"No," said old Mr. Dodd, "no more than I doubt the safety of Him who said when He was dying, *My God, why hast thou forsaken me?*" (Matthew 27:46).

Full assurance is not of the essence of salvation.

* * * *

- **Despair** of spirit leaves when you lean hard on the Cross-Bearer.

- *Deus vult:* God wills it – is a grand cry to produce a crusade.

- **Do not** please the devil by distrusting your faithful God.

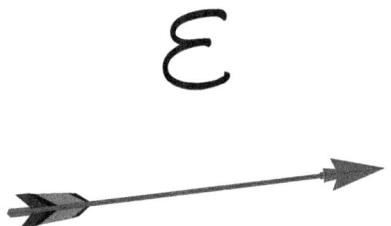

Earthly joys: The joys of this life are like the ice palace of Montreal. It is good to look at while the winter lasts, but it all melts away as the spring comes on. All things around us here are myths and dreams. This is the land of daydreams and shadows.

Earthly things, degrading: Do not slice pieces out of your manhood and then hope to fill up the vacancies with banknotes. He who loses manliness or godliness to gain gold cheats himself. Keep yourselves entire for God and for His Christ, and let all other matters be additions rather than subtractions. Live above the world. Its goods will come to you when you do not bid high for them. If you hunt the butterfly of wealth too eagerly, you may spoil it by the stroke with which you secure it. When earthly things are sought for as the main object, they are degraded into rubbish, and the seeker of them has fallen to be a mere man with a muckrake, turning over a dunghill to find nothing. Set your hearts on nobler things than self.

Ebb-and-flow Christians: With a great many people, is not the Christian life very much like the condition of the sea? The sea advances and gains gradually upon the beach. You would think it was about to inundate the land, but after it has reached its highest point, it retires, and so it spends its force in perpetual ebb and flow. Are not ebb-and-flow Christians as common as seashells?

Effects of evil fellowship: "Look," said a wife to her husband, "how can you drink at the rate you do? Even a hog would not do so."

The wretched man replied, "No, I do not suppose that it would. It would be more sensible than I am, no doubt; but if there was another hog at the other side of the trough that said, 'I will drink to your health,' this hog would be obliged to do the same; and if there were half a dozen together, and they kept on toasting one another, I expect the hog would get as drunk as I am."

Sad are the effects of evil fellowship.

Efficacy of earthly prayer: A lady was once at an evening party and there met with Caesar Malan, the famous pastor and theologian of Geneva. In his usual manner, he inquired of her whether she was a Christian. She was startled, surprised, and bothered, and made a short reply to the effect that it was not a question she cared to discuss. Mr. Malan then replied with great sweetness that he would not persist in speaking of it, but that he would pray that she might be led to give her heart to Christ and become a useful worker for Him.

Within a couple weeks, she met the minister again and asked him how she must come to Jesus. Mr. Malan's reply was, "Come to Him just as you are." The lady gave herself up to Jesus. The lady was Charlotte Elliot, to whom we owe that precious hymn:

> Just as I am, without one plea
>   But that Thy blood was shed for me,
> And that Thou bidd'st me come to Thee,
>   O Lamb of God, I come!

It was a blessed thing for her that she was at that party and that the servant of God from Geneva was there who spoke to her so faithfully.

Encouragement: You remember the story of the man who had a good wife, and someone said to him, "Why, she is worth her weight in gold."

"Yes," he said, "she is worth a Gibraltar rock in gold, but I never tell her that. You know that it is necessary to maintain discipline, and if I were to tell her how much I really value her, she would not know herself."

Well, now, that is wrong. It does people good to be told how highly we value them. There are many Christian men and women who would do better if someone would speak a kind word to them every once in a while and let them know they had done well.

Encouragement, gentle: What trouble some of us used to have when we got up in the morning and had to strike a light in the old-fashioned way. There we were with a flint and a steel, striking away in a tiresome manner until we saw a little spark down in the tinder. Oh, it was such a little spark, and then we gently tried to blow it into a flame! How we used to prize a spark on a cold, frosty morning when our fingers were pretty well frozen! We never put out sparks by shutting the lid on the top of the tinder, but we tried to light our match if we could. Well, the Lord Jesus will blow upon you with the soft breath of His love until the little spark rises into a flame.

End strife, death is near: I remember well the story of a husband who had upset his wife. I do not know what had happened – some little awkward word or deed. He went out of the house. He had to fell timber that day, and he turned back and said, "Wife, I am very sorry. Let us part good friends. Give me a kiss." Sadly, she turned away! All day long she sorrowed, for she loved him well, and she grieved to think that he was gone without that kiss of love. What's more, he never came back alive. Four men brought him home a corpse. She would have given a thousand worlds if they had not parted so.

Do not part with anyone you love with any kind of argument or quarrel. End all that, for death is near. If there is but a step between you and death (1 Samuel 20:3) – if the judge is at the door – then go and wind up your little difficulties. You who have family quarrels, wipe them out. You who have any malice in your hearts, get rid of it.

Endurance to the end: After Sir Francis Drake had sailed around the world, he came up the Thames River, and when he had passed Gravesend there came a storm that threatened the ship. The brave commander said, "What! Go around the world safely, and then get drowned in a ditch? Never!" So we should say that God has upheld us in great tribulations, and we are not going to be cast down by trials that are common to men.

Endurance wins: It is said that the French had courage enough on the spur of the moment to have rushed up to the cannon's mouth, but that the German was the victor because he could quietly abide the heat of the battle; when things looked bleak, he steadfastly kept his post. In the long run, perseverence is the winning virtue. *He that shall endure unto the end, the same shall be saved* (Mark 13:13). He who can wait with hope is the person who fights with courage.

Eternal life, a free gift: I have heard that a missionary who was trying to make an Oriental understand salvation by grace tried to explain it in many ways to him and failed, until at last he cried, "Salvation is a *baksheesh* of the Almighty." Then the Easterner understood the idea. Eternal life is the free gift of God that He bestows on men, not because of anything in them or anything that they have done, felt, or promised, but because of His own infinite goodness and the delight that He has in showing mercy.

Evil company: You have your comfort and joy; refuse to be robbed of them. If you were in a room and had your watch with you, and you saw a certain number of gentlemen of a suspicious character, you would not feel it necessary to stop and see whether they were able to extract your watch from you, but you would say to yourself, "No, it is better for me to leave this company." We are safest out of the society of those whose great object it is to rob us of our faith.

Evil conquered: The very easiest way to give resurrection to old corruptions is to erect a trophy over their graves. They will at once lift up their heads and shout out, "We are still alive." It is a great thing to overcome any sinful habit, but it is still necessary to guard against, for you have not conquered it as long as you congratulate yourself upon the conquest.

Evil turned to good: I once had a friend who was an upright, gracious man, a gentleman whom God had prospered. When employed at a bank, he had acted uprightly in a matter in which his superiors had judged him to be conscientiously foolish, and therefore they dismissed him. He could not do wrong, so he was left with a wife and family, without a job, and as everybody told him, he was hopelessly ruined because of his "foolish conscience."

But now, for years, he has been the head of that very bank. In a remarkable way, the Lord made his initial dismissal the means of his advancement, so that he rose step-by-step to be the master, where he had been the rejected servant. Humanly speaking, this would not have come about if it had not been for the incident mentioned. Have faith that God can turn the evil into good, and that which threatens to annihilate you will be the means of your increase.

Excess in right: A little excess in the right may be wrong. It may be wise to look, but foolish to gaze. There is a very thin line sometimes between that which is commendable and that which is condemnable. There is a golden middle that is not easy to keep. There is a gazing that is not commendable when the look becomes not that of reverent worship, but of an excessive curiosity, when the desire to know what should be known is mingled with prying into that which it is for God's glory to conceal.

Experience: When freshwater sailors first go to sea, every capful of wind frightens them. If the vessel lurches a little, they cry, "She will certainly go over!" However, the old sailor, who knows what a storm means, thanks God for the wind, for it will drive the ship more rapidly into port, and he never minds a lurch or two, for he has his sea legs by this time. In the same way, people who have been blessed by God for years should be equally at ease.

Experience, my own: An unbeliever once sneered at a poor woman, and said, "How do you know the Bible is true?"

She answered, "I have experienced the truth of it."

He replied, "Your experience has nothing to do with me."

"No," she said, "that's very likely, but it has everything to do with me."

And so it is. My experience may not convince another person, but my experience has rooted, grounded, and settled myself.

Experience teaches: A boy climbed into a neighbor's garden and stole some unripe plums, and after eating them, he became very ill and was forced to drink pints of horrible medicine to save his life. When he was better, his classmates said to him, "Come with us and steal some plums," but they seemed to be mocking him. The boy is very upright, is he not? He remembers the moans and pains that those plums brought him, and he wants no more of them. The child who has been burned dreads the fire. Thus the Lord often brings His people away from their sins by giving them sharp, bitter experiences of what sin will do to them.

External religion: At sea, the dredge brings up innumerable creeping things, and among them creatures that have their own natural shell to live in. However, here comes a man who has taken the shell of a large sea creature and carries it around as if it were his own. He lives in it while it suits him, and he gives up the occupancy when it becomes inconvenient. The shell is not part of himself. Avoid such a religion. Beware of a Sunday shell and a weekday without the shell. The religion that you can part with, you had better part with. If you can get rid of it, get rid of it. If it is not a part and parcel of yourself, it is good for nothing. If it does not run right through you like a silver thread through a piece of embroidery, it will not profit you in regard to your eternal salvation.

Extremity, God's opportunity: If we still have a batch of dough in the kneading bowl that we brought out of Egypt, the windows of heaven will not yet be opened; but when the last little cake has been baked, the manna will fall around the camp. As long as we can feel the bottom of the river, we have not reached the best water to swim in. When the barley loaves and the few small fishes are all broken, then the miracle of multiplying begins.

* * * *

- Empty buckets are the most suitable buckets for the well of grace.

- Every ungodly man may have his life lease run out tomorrow.

- Every day, wear the red cross on your arm by affirming your faith in the atoning blood.

- Everything it will honestly bear, you may pile upon the back of a divine promise.

- Every believer in the cross must bear the cross.

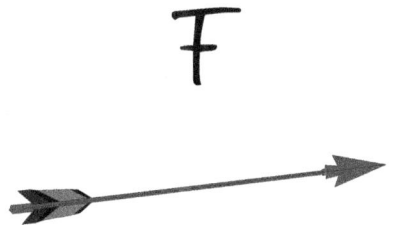

Faith: When William Huntington wrote his *Bank of Faith*, some people called it a *Bank of Nonsense*. I could write twenty *Banks of Faith*, and every word would be as sure as an honest man could write; but the only result would be that the world would say, "Oh, well, you know, that is the result of the good man's fanaticism." The moment that the moderns do not like to believe something, they call it fanatical.

Faith and repentance: Which is first: the new birth, faith, or repentance? Nobody can say which spoke of a wheel moves first, for it moves as a whole. The moment the divine life comes into the heart, we believe. The moment we believe, the eternal life is there. We repent because we believe, and we believe while we repent.

Faith casts out doubt: I am like the good man and his wife who had kept a lighthouse for years. A visitor who came to see the lighthouse looked out from the window over the waste of waters and asked the good woman, "Are you not afraid of a night when the storm is out and the big waves dash right over the lantern? Do you not fear that the lighthouse and all that is in it will be carried away?" The woman remarked that the idea never occurred to her. She had lived there so long that she felt as safe on the lone rock as ever she did when she lived on the mainland.

As for her husband, when asked if he did not feel anxious when the wind blew a hurricane, he answered, "Yes, I feel anxious to keep the lamps well trimmed and the light burning lest any vessel should be wrecked." As to anxiety about the safety of the lighthouse or his own personal security in it, he had outlived all that.

That is how it is with me: *I know whom I have believed, and am persuaded that he is able to keep that which I have committed unto him against that day* (2 Timothy 1:12). From this point on, let no one trouble me with doubts and questionings. I bear in my soul the proofs of the Spirit's truth and power, and I will not consider any of their slippery reasonings. The gospel to me is truth. I am content to perish if it is not true. I risk my soul's eternal fate upon the truth of the gospel, and I know no risk in it. My one concern is to keep the lamps burning so that I may thereby enlighten others. Only let the Lord give me oil enough to feed my lamp so that I may cast a ray of light across the dark and treacherous sea of life, and I am well content.

Faith in the commander: The ship is on fire. The bales of cotton are pouring forth a black, horrible smoke. Passengers and crew are in extreme danger, but a capable captain is in command, and he says to those around him, "If you will behave yourselves, I think I will be able to bring about the safety of everyone." If they trust in the captain, they will do precisely as he orders. No sailor or engineer will refuse to work the pumps or prepare the boats. No passenger will disobey any rule. In proportion to their confidence in their leader will be the willingness with which they obey him at once. They believe his orders to be wise, so they adhere to them. Neither their fear nor their impulsiveness will lead them to rush to and fro contrary to his instructions if they have a firm trust in him.

When the boats are lowered and are brought one by one to the ship's side, those who are to fill them wait until their turns come – in firm reliance upon the captain's impartiality and prudence. They will get into the boats or they will wait on board, for they consider that his orders are dictated by a better judgment than their own. As far as each man and each woman firmly believes in the superior officer, discipline will be maintained.

Faith in the promises: A person comes to the bank with a check. He believes it to be honestly his and believes that the signature is correct. He puts it down on the counter, and the clerk gives him the money. But then the man does not take it. He stands and waits. The clerk looks at him and wonders what he is up to. At last, when the person has been there long enough to wear the good man's patience out, the clerk says, "Did you bring the check to have the money?"

"Yes, I handed you the check."

"Well, then, why don't you take the money and go about your business?"

If he is a sensible man, he will delay no longer. If he were sensible, he would not have delayed so long. He takes the money and departs in peace. Now dear soul, if you have a promise from God – *He that believeth on him is not condemned* (John 3:18), or *He that believeth on the Son hath everlasting life* (John 3:36) – do you believe? Then take the blessing and go about your business.

Faith must be used: Did you ever hear of a captain of a ship that was being driven about by rough winds who wanted to drop his anchor and desired to drop the anchor somewhere on board the ship where it would hold fast? He hangs it at the bow of the ship, but still the ship moves on. He places the anchor upon deck, but that does not hold the vessel. At last he puts it down into the hold, but with no better success.

Anchors do not hold as long as they are on board a ship. They must be thrown into the deep, and then they will get a grip of the sea bottom and hold the vessel against wind and tide. As long as you have confidence in yourself, you are like a man who keeps his anchor on board his boat, and you will never come to a resting place. Cast your faith over into the great deeps of eternal love and power, and trust in the infinitely faithful One.

Faith, not feeling: Suppose that there is a ship out at sea, and those on board feel they are safe. One of them says, "I know we will not drift far out of our course because we have such a big anchor on board."

You say, "Ah, he is not very wise. He must be a fool who believes in an anchor on board."

It is no good to anybody. It is when you let the anchor go and lose sight of it, and the anchor gets an unseen grip down below, that it is good for something; but while the anchor is on board, it is only dead weight on the ship. You want to have your anchor on board, do you not? You do not like it to enter that which is within the veil and that which is too mysterious. You want to feel something, to have something of your own.

Faith, practical: Multitudes of people have a kind of faith in God, but it does not come to the practical point of trusting that God will deliver them. I see in the newspaper advertisements, "Startling news! People in the planets!" That is not a very practical discovery. For a while now there has been a tendency to refer God's promises and our faith to the planets, or somewhere beyond this present everyday life. We say to ourselves, "Oh, yes, God delivers His people." We mean that He did so in the days of Moses, and possibly He may be doing so now on some obscure island of the sea. The glory of faith lies in its being suitable for everyday wear.

Faith subdues fear: I knew a youth nearly forty years ago who was staying with relatives when a thunderstorm of unusual violence came on at nightfall. A haystack was struck by lightning and set on fire within sight of the door. The grown-up people in the house, both men and women, were completely overcome with fright. The strong men seemed even more afraid than the women. All the residents of the house sat huddled together. Only this youth was quietly happy.

There was a little child upstairs in bed, and the mother was concerned about him, but even her love could not give her courage enough to pass the staircase windows to bring that child down. The baby cried, and this youth, who was then recently converted, went upstairs alone, took the child, and without hurry or alarm, brought him down to his mother. He needed no candle, for the lightning was so continuous that he could see his way quite well. He felt that the Lord was wonderfully near that night, and so no fear was possible to his heart. He sat down and read a psalm aloud to his trembling relatives, who looked on the lad with loving wonder.

That night he was master of the situation, and those in the house believed that there was something in the religion that he had so recently professed. I believe that if all of us can, by God's grace, get such a sense of God's nearness to us in times of danger and trouble that we remain calm, we will bring much honor to the cause of God and the name of Jesus.

Faith, taught by nature: Mungo Park (1771-1806), the African traveler, lost his way in the wilds, and there and then was comforted by viewing a tiny moss and noticing its remarkable beauty. He saw the finger of God in that small object, and he felt sure that God would take care of him. So may we be taught faith by every created thing – that the Creator can do all things.

Faith, the certainty of hope: When I had found Christ and joined the church, I began to teach in the Sunday school, but my little class of boys taught me more than I taught them. I was speaking to them one day about Mark 16:16, *He that believeth and is baptized shall be saved*, and one of the boys said to me, "Teacher, have you been baptized?"

"Yes."

"Then you are saved, teacher?" he asked.

"I hope so."

The boy looked me straight in the face and said, "And don't you know, teacher?"

I replied, "Yes, I do know it."

"Of course," said the boy. "The text says so. If it ain't true, it ain't true, and if it is true, it is true, and nobody needs to hope about it."

So it was. The boy used good logic. The Scripture says, *He that believeth and is baptized shall be saved*. Therefore, he who believes and is baptized is saved.

Faith, the greatest ability: In the school of grace, faith is the greatest ability by which we make advances in wisdom. If by faith you have been able to say, "A and B and C," it must be by faith that you will go on to say, "D and E and F," until you will arrive at the end of the alphabet and become an expert in the book of wisdom. If by faith you can read in the spelling book of simple faith, then by the same faith in Christ Jesus, you must go on to read in the classics of full assurance and become a scribe well instructed in the things of the kingdom. Therefore, keep close to the practice of faith, from which so many are turning aside.

Faith, the queen bee: The other day, I saw my bees swarming. They hung on a branch of a tree in a living mass. The difficulty was to get them into a hive. My man went with his veil over his face and began to put them into the hive. I noticed that he was especially desirous to get the queen bee into it, for once he had her in the hive, the rest would be sure to follow and remain with her. Faith is the queen bee. You may get self-control, love, hope, and all those other bees into the hive, but the main thing is to get simple faith in Christ, and all the rest will come afterward. Get the queen bee of faith, and all the other virtues will join her.

Faith, to be used: God never gave us faith to play with. It is a sword, but it was not made for presentation on a gala day, nor to be worn on state occasions only, nor to be exhibited upon a parade ground. It is a sword that was meant to cut and wound and slay, and he who carries it about him may expect, between here and heaven, that he will know what battle means. Faith is a sound, seagoing vessel, and was not meant to lie in dock and perish of dry rot. To whom God has given faith, it is as though one gave a lantern to his friend because he expected it to be dark on his way home. The very gift of faith is a hint to you that you will need it, that at certain points and places you will especially require it, and that at all points and in every place you will really need it.

Faithfulness: You know what the old manservant said in the olden time when his master angrily said, "We must part, John."

"I hope not, sir. Where are you going?" He had no intention of leaving his master.

"Ah!" said his master, "I do not intend to employ you any longer."

The old servant is said to have answered, "Sir, if you do not have a good servant, I know that I have a good master, and I do not intend to leave him. I cannot think of going away."

It is a great thing to feel that you are not going away from God – that you have such a good Master that you are going to cling to the posts of His door; and if He puts you out by the front door, you intend to come in at the back. Let the Lord do what He pleases. I am forever bound to belong to Him only. Brother, resolve that if you cannot preach for your Lord, you will hear for Him; and if you cannot be a leader of the church, you will be a follower somewhere – but resolve to serve your Lord forever.

False confidence: Some trust in horses (Psalm 20:7). You may have fine horses of morality and religiousness. You may have many virtues upon which you think you might fairly depend. Give up these trusts. Have you recently been trotting out your horses before your whole family, and saying to your wife, "I am not like many men. I never drink too much, and I do not treat my household unkindly"? Put away these horses. You cannot come to God riding on pride. Say, "We will not ride upon horses." Put away every confidence in yourself in whatever manner it appears.

Familiarity breeds neglect: I am told that the good people in the valley of Ohio, whose houses have been swept away by the tornado, had a warning that the storm was coming. The storm drums were out, and newspapers announced there was a great storm coming their way. They did not take any notice of that information. It did not seem very threatening. They were used to paragraphs in the paper. If it was only once a year that the weather could be fairly predicted, we would want to buy the gazette that day, but now since we get it every morning, we do not take any notice of it. These poor Ohio friends took no notice and were by no means prepared for the storm. Familiarity breeds neglect.

Fear about your future: When a large vessel is crossing the sea and another comes within sight, they propose the question, "Where are you bound?" If the other vessel took no notice and gave no answer whatsoever, it would look suspicious. We do not like the looks of a ship that will not say where it is going. If one of Her Majesty's vessels were about, and it challenged a sail and received no reply to the question, "Where are you bound?" I think they would fire a shot across her bows and make her heave to until she answered. Could not the silent vessel prove to be a pirate ship?

When a man confesses that he does not know where he is going or what his business is, the policeman concludes that he is probably going where he should not go and that he has business on hand that is not right. If you are afraid to consider your future, your fear is a bad sign. The tradesman who is afraid to look into his accounts will, before long, have them looked into for him by an officer from the Bankruptcy Court. He who dares not see his own face in the mirror must be an ugly fellow, and you who dare not behold your character have a bad character.

Fear of man: Think of a king saying, "I am afraid." However, that is what the French king said to Bernard Palissy, the potter. As nearly as I can remember the story, the monarch said, "Palissy, you must go to mass."

"That I never will," he answered.

"Then I am afraid I will have to give you up to be burnt."

"There," said Palissy, "your Majesty could never make me say such a word as that, with all your power. I am no king, only a poor potter, but nobody made me say, 'I am afraid.'"

Oh, that wretched fear of men, that dread of ridicule, that wishing to avoid sarcasm! How it has made men come down from the dignity of their office, from the honor of the position that God has conferred upon them, and has made them lower than the servants around them.

Floral preaching: Many are the floral displays in sermons. Sheaves of corn are too plain and rustic. This is the age of bouquets and wreaths of rare flowers. Paul must give way to Browning, and David to Tennyson. There are enough in the novelty business without us, and we have something better to do. We have to give an account unto our God of what we do and say, and if we have been murderers of souls, it will be no excuse that we brandished the dagger well, or that when we gave them poison, we mixed the drink cleverly and presented it with poetic phrases.

Food, Christ our: A man is made by that which he feeds upon, and for the best manhood, you need the best food. Certain silkworms have their silk colored by the leaves on which they feed, and if we were to feed on Christ, and nothing else but Christ, we would become pure, holy, lowly, meek, gentle, and humble; in a word, we would be perfect, even as He is (Matthew 5:48).

Food, heavenly: There are different theories about what we should eat. One person tells us that if anyone suffers from rheumatism, he must eat so many pounds of meat in a day. Other doctors have vehemently said, "You must not touch meat. It will hurt you if you do. You must keep to a strictly vegetable diet." I believe that these educated people each know as much as the other about it, and probably all of them put together know so little that a very small round zero might encompass all their certain knowledge as to health and disease.

However, there is one thing we do know – that the bread that the Israelites ate in the wilderness, the manna, was the best kind of food. It was God's own invention, and He who created man knew best what nourishment his life would require. It was not enhanced bread, but it was celestial bread that had never been soured with earthly leaven. It had dropped directly from the sky – the best food that men could eat if they wanted to be healthy, active, and able to endure a hard and toilsome life.

Forces, God-hidden: Our royal Leader has hidden forces at His command. Sir Walter Scott speaks of the Highland chieftain in the lone glen who gave his shrill whistle, and an army immediately arose where none had been seen before.

> From the shingles gray their lances start,
> The bracken bush sends forth the dart,
> The rushes and the willow wand,
> Are bristling into axe and brand,
> And every tuft of broom gives life
> To plaided warrior armed for strife.[2]
> Thus can our Lord gather His church in a moment.

Form, the leaves of: When tea was first introduced into this country, someone gave a friend a gift of a pound of it. It was exceedingly expensive, and when he met his friend next, he inquired, "Have you tried the tea?"

"Yes, but I did not like it at all."

"How was that? Everybody else is enraptured with it."

"Well," said the other, "we boiled it in a saucepan, threw away the water, and brought the leaves to the table; but nobody cared for them."

In the same way, many people keep the leaves of form and throw away the spiritual meaning.

Freed from sin: I saw two men yesterday handcuffed and marched to the carriage to be taken off to prison. They could not move their wrists. Suppose, though, that I had walked behind them with my wrists close

---

2   This is from "The Lady of the Lake," a poem by Sir Walter Scott (1771-1832).

together and had never opened my hands nor moved them, and said, "Alas! Many years ago I committed some wrong, and had handcuffs put upon me."

You would naturally say, "Well, but are they not taken off?"

I would reply, "Yes, I have heard they are, but somehow, through habit, I go around as if I had them on."

Everybody would say of me, "That man must be insane!" Now you, child of God, once had the handcuffs on. Your sins were upon you, but Jesus Christ took them off. When you believed in Him, He broke all your chains, and now they are not there.

Fruitless action: Under the influence of great love, we may act unwisely. I well remember seeing the action of a woman whose only son was emigrating to a distant colony. I stood in the station, and I noticed her many tears and her frequent embraces of the boy, but the train arrived and he entered the carriage. After the train had passed beyond the station, she was foolish enough to break away from friends who sought to detain her. She ran along the platform, leaped down upon the railroad tracks, and pursued the speeding train. It was natural, but it had been better left undone. We had better abstain from acts that serve no practical purpose, for in this life, we have neither time nor strength to waste in fruitless action.

Future state: I truly believe that if we could see ourselves as we will be, it would make us laugh for very joy. If we could look in some supernatural mirror in which we could see ourselves in the glorified state, we would sit down and look at it with amazement until we would ask, "Can that be me? Is it possible that I will ever come to such glory and beauty?" O my brother, you are only in the egg as yet; you have chipped a little bit of it, and you have looked out, but the most that you have seen is your own shell. Do you not know that you have wings? Yes, they are wings that you cannot stretch yet, for they are limited by the shell, but you will soon spread them and rise up into that clear blue where eagles are at home. You will rise above all visible things and reach the serene abodes of the blessed.

* * * *

- Faith gathers the handfuls of sacred corn from which contemplation threshes out the ears and prepares soul-sustaining bread.

- Faith is a salamander that lives in the fire, a star that moves in a lofty sphere, a diamond that bores its way through the rock.

- Faith is the acorn from which the oak of holiness will grow.

- Faith is the fountain, the foundation, and the fosterer of obedience.

- Faith is the mother of holiness and the nurse of virtue.

- Faith knows that whenever she gets a dark envelope from the heavenly post office, there is a treasure in it.

- Faith laughs at that which fear weeps over.

- Faith must be a constant tenant, not an occasional guest.

- Faith sees sweet love in every bitter cup.

- Fanaticism is a tornado of the flesh.

- Full assurance is the Koh-i-noor diamond among the jewels wherewith the heavenly Bridegroom adorns His spouse.

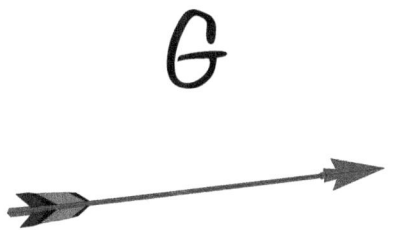

Giving, generous: I remember that when I was able to journey through the country preaching, I occasionally stayed with a fine old English farmer. He used to have a piece of beef upon the table. I do not know how many pounds it weighed, but it was enormous. I said to him one day, "Why is it that whenever I come here you have such immense portions of meat? Do you think that I can eat like a giant? If so, it is a great mistake. Look at that portion there. If I were to take it home, it might last me a month."

"Well," he said, "if I could get a bigger piece, I would, for I am so glad to see you; and if you could eat it all, you would be heartily welcome to do so. I want everybody who comes here today to feel that I will do my very best for you."

He did not measure my necessities to the half-ounce, but he provided on a lavish scale. I quote this simple example of giving generously to show you how the Lord makes ready for His guests on a divine scale.

Giving, manner of: There is a way of turning a coin into stone or into gold, according to the way in which you give it to a poor man. You can fling it at him as if he were a dog, and he will be about as grateful to you as a dog, or not so much. But there is a way in which you can say, "I am sorry for your needs. This is all I can afford now. Take it and do what you can with it." Given with a brotherly look, it will be gratefully received and made the most of. There is much in the manner as well as in the matter of the gift. The mannerism of Christ is wondrously gracious. He saves us rejoicingly.

Gladness: You have heard machinery at times complaining miserably. It has gone on with horrible gratings and creakings. It has set your teeth on edge. Get the oil can! We must fix this grinding. Every now and then we need a few drops of the oil of gladness to make the wheels of our work move pleasantly. Men of the world teach us the value of joyous song. How easily the anchor rises when the sailors unite in cheerful cries! When soldiers are weary on the march, they find their spirits revived when the band strikes up a stirring tune. Let it be so today. Praise God with the sound of the trumpet (Psalm 150:3). Let the children of Zion rejoice in their King (Psalm 149:2).

Glory in humility: When Sapor, the great Persian, jested with a Jew about his Messiah riding upon a donkey, he said to him, "I will send Him one of my horses."

The rabbi replied, "You cannot send Him a horse that will be good enough, for that donkey is to be of a hundred colors."

By that idle tradition, the rabbi showed that he had not understood the idea of the prophet at all, since he could not believe in Messiah's lowliness displayed by his riding upon a common donkey. The rabbinical mind must necessarily make simplicity mysterious and turn lowliness into another form of extravagance and show. The very heart of the matter is that our Lord gave Himself no grand airs, but was natural, simple, and free from all pride. His greatest pomp went no further than riding through Jerusalem upon a colt, the foal of a donkey.

The Muslim turns around with a sneer and says to the Christian, "Your Master rode on a donkey; our Mohammed rode on a camel, and the camel is by far the superior beast." That is true, and that is where the Muslim fails to grasp the prophetic thought. He looks for strength and honor, but Jesus triumphs by weakness and humility. How little glory is to be found in the grandeur and display that princes of this world adopt! There is far more true glory in condescension than in display.

Glory of the Lord: Have you ever heard how the Laplanders climb the hills when the sun is at last about to appear after the weary winter months? Have you heard how they rejoice in the first beams of the rising sun? In the same way, let us rise to lofty meditation and look to our Lord and Master until we perceive His mediatorial glory and are blessed thereby. Have you no time? Give up your newspaper for a week so that you may sanctify the time to the noble end of considering the glory of your Lord, and I will guarantee that you will get a thousand times more out of such thought than from skimming the daily journal. Look unto Jesus, and the light within will grow like the glory of heaven.

God everywhere: I remember once visiting a poor Christian in the hospital who had often heard me preach, and he said, "Sir, you have given us so many illustrations that, as I lie in bed, everything I see, hear, or read brings to mind something in your sermons." How much more true is this of our Great Teacher! We are glad that He has hung up the gospel everywhere, until every dewdrop reflects Him and every wind whispers His name. Day and night talk to each other of Him, and the hours commune concerning things to come.

God first, methods second: We often stop at the methods and begin to calculate their natural force, and thus we miss our mark. The point is to get beyond the instruments to the God who uses the instruments. I have heard that a wax candle fired from a rifle will go through a door; the penetrating power is not in the candle, but in the force propelling it. We are nothing, but God with us is everything. *He giveth power to the faint; and to them that have no might he increaseth strength* (Isaiah 40:29).

God lives: While God lives, truth is in the ascendant. I remember years ago meeting with that blessed servant of God, the late Earl of Shaftesbury. He was at Mentone with a dying daughter, and he happened that day to be very much downcast – as, indeed, I have frequently seen him, and, as I am sorry to confess, he has also frequently seen me. That day he was especially discouraged about the general state of society. He thought that the powers of darkness in this country were having it all their own way, and that before long, the worst elements of society would gain power and trample out all virtue. Looking up into his face, I said to him, "And is God dead? Do you believe that while God lives, the devil will conquer Him?"

He smiled, and we walked along by the Mediterranean Sea communing together in a far more hopeful tone. *The LORD liveth; and blessed be my rock* (Psalm 18:46). As long as the Lord lives, our hope lives also. Gospel truth will still prevail. We will live to see the old faith at the forefront again. The church, like Noah's dove, will come back to her rest again and will bring with her something that will prophesy eternal peace.

"God make me new": I think it was Charles I who used to swear, "God mend me." Somebody said it would be an easier job to make a new one of him, and I believe it. When people say, "God mend me," they had better say, "God make me new."

God, never weary: I had a dear friend whose company I enjoyed, but all of a sudden he stopped coming to see me. He stayed away, and as I knew he had not ceased to love me, I wondered why. I eventually learned that the good brother had gotten it into his head that he might outrun his welcome. He had read those words of Solomon, *Withdraw thy foot from thy neighbor's house; lest he be weary of thee, and so hate thee* (Proverbs 25:17). I admired my friend's caution, but I worked hard to make him see that Solomon knew nothing about me, and that I was more wearied when he stayed away than when he came. I hope he made me an exception to a very sensible rule.

Never, though, get that thought into your head concerning your God. *Will ye weary my God also?* (Isaiah 7:13). You may weary Him by praying less, but never by abounding in supplication. Abide with your God and cry to Him day and night, and let this be the music of your whole life, *whereunto I may continually resort* (Psalm 71:3).

God or gold: Apparent zeal for God may really be zeal for gold. Emperor Maximilian showed great zeal against idolatry and published a decree that gold and silver images should be melted down. He was extremely zealous about this. The images were all to be melted down and the metal forfeited to the emperor. It was shrewdly suspected that this great iconoclast was not altogether swayed by unselfish motives. When a business brings grist to the mill, it is not hard to keep to it. Some love Christ because they carry His bag for Him (see John 12:6).

God's delight in us: A little baby, if he had understanding and could look at himself, would say, "How inferior I am to my father! What feeble hands! What tottering feet! I am a poor, puny, dependent creature." Yes, but that is not the way the mother thinks of him. She sees a loveliness in the weakness and a beauty in the littleness of her baby. She looks at him until her eyes swim with tears lest anything should harm him. She thinks he is the most beautiful thing that ever was, and doubtless he is so to her.

Our God has all the instincts of motherhood and fatherhood blended in one, and when He looks upon His church, He calls her *Hephzibah*: "My delight is in her" (Isaiah 62:4). I do not read that He delights in the works of nature alone, but He rejoices *in the habitable part of his earth* (Proverbs 8:31). He does not rejoice in the works of His hands as much as in the works of His heart. The whole Godhead is at home in blessing those whom everlasting love has ordained to everlasting life.

God's help in daily life: I am reminded of Henry Havelock and his saints in the Indian Mutiny. There was a stern fight to be fought, and the general said, "Send for Havelock and his saints," and they soon accomplished the task. When you get men who thoroughly serve Christ in whatever position of life they are, they are formidable fellows. They will do the thing where others will only talk about it. God does indeed help those who put their trust in Him, in the ordinary concerns of daily life.

God's watchmen, Christians: In times of war, every fortified city had upon its walls certain watchmen so as to see eye to eye. That is to say, the eye of one sentinel reached to the eye of another, and so they encompassed the city all the way around. The sentinels challenged whoever passed that way by day or night. If he happened to be an enemy, they sounded an alarm and soldiers immediately came forth from the guardroom, and the city was protected against a surprise attack. God's people – especially the stronger, the more instructed, and the most experienced of them – should act as watchmen on the walls, for Christ's sake.

God's watchmen, ministers: We are not set to keep the church of God by day only, but we are also to maintain our watch amid the dews and frosts of the darkest night. Christians are to be sentries who will not retreat into the barracks because of the cold, nor leave the rampart because of the heat. Watchmen are most required at night. We are to be *instant in season* (2 Timothy 4:2), giving the password at each different time when the watch reports itself, and thus never holding our peace day or night. We are to be instant *out of season*, for at such times the enemy is most likely to come. God's watchmen are not on duty by the hour to watch by turns, but they are bound to be watchers for souls throughout life. We are never off duty. We take a day and night shift. Our rest is in the Lord's service; our recreation is in change of occupation.

God's Word to be believed: John Locke, the great philosopher, spent the last fourteen years of his life in the study of the Bible, and when asked what was the quickest way for a young gentleman to understand the Christian religion, he urged him to read the Bible, remarking, "Therein are contained the words of eternal life. It has God for its author, salvation for its end, and truth, without any admixture of error, for its matter."

There are those on the side of God's Word whom you need not to be ashamed of in the matter of intelligence and learning, and if it were not so, it should not discourage you when you remember that the Lord has *hid these things from the wise and prudent, and hast revealed them unto babes* (Matthew 11:25). We believe with the apostle that *the foolishness of God is wiser than men* (1 Corinthians 1:25). It is better to believe what comes out of God's mouth and be called a fool than to believe what comes out of the mouth of philosophers and be considered a wise man.

God with His saints: As the heavens stand unbraced and unsupported except by the Word of God, so stands the man of God. Martin Luther realized this, and when they said that Duke George would oppose him, he said, "If it rained Duke Georges, I would not care, as long as I have God with me."

> Fear Him, ye saints, and you will then
> Have nothing else to fear;
> Make you His service your delight,
> He'll make your wants His care.[3]

---

3 This is a stanza from a hymn written by Nahum Tate (1652-1715) that begins with "Through all the changing scenes of life."

Good news: The first missionaries to Greenland thought that the natives were too debased to understand the doctrine of atonement right away, so they began to tell them of the existence of a God, and so on. No effect was produced by such common information. However, when translating the chapter of John in which the passage occurs, *God so loved the world, that he gave his only begotten Son, that whosoever believeth in him should not perish, but have everlasting life* (John 3:16), a Greenlander asked, "Is that true?" When the missionary affirmed that it was, he said, "Why, then, did you not tell us that at first, for that is good news indeed?"

Good soldiers: Two things are desired in a good soldier: steadiness under fire and enthusiasm during a charge. The first is the more essential in most battles, for victory often depends upon the power of endurance that makes a battalion of men into a wall of brass. We need the dashing courage that can carry a position by storm; that will be used up in the second characteristic – *always abounding in the work of the Lord* (1 Corinthians 15:58).

Gospel, a gun: The gospel is our *Mons Meg*, the biggest gun in the castle. It is not out of date, though, for it will carry a ball far enough to reach the heart of the sinner who is furthest from God. Satan trembles when he hears the roar of the gospel gun. Let it never be silent.

Gospel, an offense to enemies: A great general going in before his king stumbled over his sword. "I see," said the king, "your sword is in the way."
    The warrior answered, "Your Majesty's enemies have often felt the same."
    That our gospel offends the King's enemies is no regret to us.

Gospel, a trumpet: It happened one evening when there was a large gathering of friends at the orphanage that our boys were sweetly playing a hymn tune upon their bells, the American organ was being played as an accompaniment, and all the gathered company were singing at their best, making a rushing flood of music. Just then I hinted to our friend, Mr. Manton Smith, to add a few notes from his silver cornet. When he placed it to his lips and threw his soul into it, the lone man was heard above us all. Bells, organ, voices, and everything seemed to yield before that one clear blast of trumpet music. So will it be with the gospel. Only sound it out as God's own Word and let the power of the Holy Spirit go with it, and it will drown all music but its own.

Gospel heard in vain: Did you ever go to a physician? Did you ever wait for an hour or two before you could see the great man? Did you give him your money? Did he hand you a prescription? Tell me, did you leave it on the table? Did you fold it up carefully and put it in your pocket? Did you keep it there? Did you not have the medicine made up? Did you not take the medicine? Suppose that in a month's time someone were to say, "Did you see the doctor?"

"Yes, I went to see him."

"Did you have a prescription?"

"He gave me a piece of paper with some writing on it, but I do not know what it was, for I cannot read Latin."

"Did you not go to the pharmacist to get your medicine?"

"No," you say, "I was satisfied with seeing the doctor."

Dear friends, you smile at this description of folly, for it is such obvious lack of wisdom. Be wise, then. Do not hear the gospel in vain by neglecting God's demands. If you know how to be saved, obey the command.

Gospel, hearing the: Remember Hugh Latimer's quaint story when he urged all his hearers to go and hear the gospel. He even praised that sleepless woman who had been taking sleeping medicine, but found that there was no drug strong enough to make her sleep, until at last she said, "If you would take me to the parish church, I know that I could go to sleep, for I have slept there every Sunday for many years." She was taken to that place of rest and was soon at peace. "Well, well," said Latimer, "it is better for her to come for sleep than to not come at all." And so I say that even if you go to the Lord's house to sleep, the Lord may awaken you to seek and find the Savior.

Gospel, necessary to be plain: When a city is to be held for a siege, it will be good for those who attend to the commissary to lay in a proportion of everything that is necessary for human comfort, and even a measure of certain luxuries; but it will be of first importance to bring in large quantities of corn. The necessities of life must be the main provision. We place these in storehouses by tons, whereas in other articles, pounds may suffice. If there is a failure of bread, what will the people do? For this reason, I feel I must preach over and over again the plain gospel of salvation by grace through faith in Christ Jesus.

Gospel, no monopolizing the: I have heard that in the old Bread Riots, when people were actually starving for bread, no word had such a terribly threatening and alarming power about it as the word "Bread!" when shouted by a starving crowd. I have read a description by someone who once heard this cry. He said he had been startled at night before by a cry of "Fire!" but when he heard the cry of "Bread, bread!" from those who were hungry, it seemed to cut him like a sword. Whatever bread had been in his possession he had to hand out at once. So it is with the gospel. Once people are aware of their need of it, there is no keeping it to ourselves.

Gospel, plain: A man said about something he wanted to make clear, "Why, it is as plain as ABC!"

"Yes," said a third party, "but the man you are talking to is DEF."

So some of our hearers seem to turn away from the Word of God. Let us explain the gospel as we may; if there is no desire in the heart, our plainest messages are lost.

Gospel, poor man's: The longer I live, the more I thank God that we have not received a classical gospel, or a mathematical gospel, or a metaphysical gospel. It is not a gospel confined to scholars and men of genius, but it is a poor man's gospel, a plowman's gospel, for that is the kind of gospel that we can live upon and die upon. It is not to us the luxury of refinement, but the staple food of life. We do not need fine words when the heart is heavy, neither do we need deep problems when we are lying upon the verge of eternity, weak in body and tempted in mind. At such times we magnify the blessed simplicity of the gospel. Jesus in the flesh made manifest becomes our soul's bread. Jesus bleeding on the cross as a substitute for sinners is our soul's drink. This is the gospel for children, and strong men need nothing more.

Gospel, the: God will still save by the gospel, only let it be the gospel in its purity. This grand old sword will cleave a man's backbone and split a rock in half. How is it that it does so little of its old conquering work? I will tell you. Do you see this scabbard of artistic work, so wonderfully elaborated? Many people keep the sword in this scabbard, and therefore its edge never gets to its work. Pull off that scabbard. Fling that fine sheath to Hades, and then see how, in the Lord's hands, that glorious two-handed sword will mow down fields of men as mowers level the grass with their scythes. There is no need to go down to Egypt for help. To invite the devil to help Christ is shameful. If it is God's will, we will see prosperity yet, when the church of God is resolved never to seek it except in God's own way.

Gospel, the: I sat yesterday with two tubes in my ears to listen to sounds that came from revolving cylinders of wax. I heard music, though I knew that no instrument was near. It was music that had been recorded months before, and now was ringing out as clearly and distinctly in my ears as it could have done if I had been present at its first sound. I heard Mr. Edison speak. He repeated a childish rhyme, and when he had finished, he called upon his friends to repeat it with him. I heard many American voices joining in that repetition. That wax cylinder was present when these sounds were made, and now it talked it all out in my ear. Then I heard Mr. Edison at work in his laboratory. He was driving nails, working on metal, and doing all sorts of things, calling for this and that with that American tone that made one know his nationality. I sat and listened, and I felt lost in the mystery.

But what of all this? What can these instruments convey to us? But oh, to sit and listen to the gospel when your ears are really opened! Then you hear God Himself at work. You hear Jesus speak. You hear His voice in suffering and in glory, and you rise up and say, "I never thought to have heard such strange things! Where have I been to be so long deaf to this? How could I neglect a gospel in which are locked up such wondrous treasures of wisdom and knowledge, such measureless depths of love and grace?" In the gospel of the Lord Jesus, God speaks into the ear of His child more music than all the harps of heaven can provide.

Gospel, the simplicity of it despised: Did you ever read Nicholas Culpepper's *Herbal*? I hope you have never taken any of the remedies that learned herbalist prescribes. In one formula you will find a dozen items, each one of them distasteful, and in many prescriptions you will find twenty or more herbs most strangely mixed together. Such were the prescriptions of still earlier times. If they did no good, they did at least confound the patient.

And what is the new gospel that is proposed to us today? It is the gospel of "culture." Culture! This, of course, is the monopoly of our superiors. It is only to be enjoyed by very refined people who have been to college and who carry inside of them a whole university, library and all. The gospel, which is made to be plain enough for wandering men, is despised for that very reason. It is too common of a teaching that Jesus Christ came into the world to save sinners. That He bore our sins in His own body on the tree (1 Peter 2:24) is rejected as an outrageous belief that is unfit for this intelligent age!

Gospel, the simple: I was struck with what someone said the other day about a certain preacher. The hearer was in deep concern of soul, and the minister preached a very pretty sermon indeed, decorated abundantly with word paintings. I scarcely know any brother who can paint as daintily as this good minister can, but this poor soul, under a sense of sin, said, "There was too much landscape, sir. I did not want landscape; I wanted salvation."

Dear friend, never crave word painting when you attend a sermon, but crave Christ. You must have Christ to be your own by faith, or you are lost. When I was seeking the Savior, I remember hearing a very good doctrinal sermon; but when it was over, I longed to tell the minister that there was a poor lad there who wanted to know how he could be saved. How I wished he had given half a minute to that subject!

Dr. Thomas Manton, who was usually a clear and full preacher of the gospel, once preached before the Lord Mayor and gave his lordship something a cut above the common citizens, and so the poorer people missed their portion. After he had finished preaching his sermon, an elderly woman cried, "Dr. Manton, I came here this morning under concern of soul, wanting a blessing, and I have not got it, for I could not understand you."

The preacher meekly replied, "May the Lord forgive me! I will not so offend again."

He had overlooked the poor and had thought mainly of the Lord Mayor. Special sermons before mayors and queens and assemblies are seldom worth a penny a thousand.

Gospel, weary of the: I heard of a flower girl who sold violets in the street and had to take the remaining ones home to her poor, miserable room every night until she said that she hated the smell of violets. She got so accustomed to them that she could not bear them. "That is strange," someone says, yet that is how some of our gospel hearers speak. I dread above anything that your nostrils should become so familiar with the sweet smell of the Rose of Sharon and the Lily of the Valley that their fragrance should become nauseous to you.

"Got it": If you can believe, you are saved. I cannot help quoting my brother Hill's expression the other day: *He that believeth on me hath everlasting life* (John 6:47). You know how he put it? He said, "H-a-t-h spells 'got it.'" So it does; it is a curious, but perfectly correct way of spelling it. If you take Christ to yourself, He will never be taken from you. Breathe the air, and the air is yours. Receive Christ, and Christ is yours, and you have attained to righteousness.

Grace apparent in action: As one of the old Puritans used to say, our graces are not apparent unless they are in exercise. When you walk through a preserve, there may be partridges and pheasants and rabbits all around you. You will not see them, though, until one flies out of his hiding or a rabbit hops in front of you. You see them in motion, but while they are quiet in the underbrush, you will not observe them. In the same way, love to Christ and all Christian virtues may lie concealed until they are called into action.

Grace at work: If you had an old house, and any friend of yours were to say, "I will build you a new house. When should I begin?" you might say, "Oh, begin next week."

At the end of the week, he has pulled down half of your old house. "Oh," you say, "this is what you call building me a new house, is it? You are causing me great loss. I wish I had never agreed to your proposal."

He replies, "You are most unreasonable. How am I to build you a new house on this spot without taking down the old one?"

And so it often happens that the grace of God does seem in its first work to make a man even worse than he was before because it reveals to him sins that he did not know were there, evils that had been concealed, and dangers never dreamed of.

Grace, doctrines of: When I read some sermons, they remind me of a piece of pasture by the roadside after a hungry horde of sheep has devoured every green thing; but when I read a solid gospel sermon of the Puritans, it reminds me of a field kept for hay, which a farmer is eventually compelled to give up to the sheep. The grass has grown almost as high as themselves, and so they lie down in it, eating and also resting. Give me the doctrines of grace, and I am in clover.

Grace finds people: Many people are like that Indian who, climbing up the mountainside pursuing game, grasped a shrub to prevent his slipping, and as its roots gave way they uncovered masses of pure silver, and thus the richest silver mine was discovered by a happy accident by one who was not looking for it. These gentiles discovered in Christ the righteousness that they needed, but which they had never dreamed of finding. This reminds us of our Lord's own parable in which the man was plowing with oxen, and suddenly the plow struck upon an unusual obstacle. He stopped the plow and turned up the soil, and he found gold! This *treasure hid in a field* (Matthew 13:44) at once won his heart, and for joy thereof he sold all that he had and bought the field. Grace finds people who otherwise would never have found grace.

Grace glides into glory: Often travelers by railway ask, "When do we pass from England into Scotland?" There is no sudden jerk in the movement of the train when the border is crossed. There is no broad boundary. You glide from one to the other and scarcely know where the boundary is. The eternal life that is in the believer glides along from grace to glory without a break.

Gratitude: The ancients had many rare stories of the gratitude of wild beasts. You remember that story of Androcles and the lion. The man was condemned to be torn to pieces by wild beasts. However, the lion to which he was cast licked his feet instead of devouring him because at some former time Androcles had extracted a thorn from the grateful creature's foot.

We have heard of an eagle who so loved a boy with whom he had played that when the child was sick, the eagle sickened, too; and when the child slept, this strange bird slept; and when the child awoke, the eagle awoke; and when the child died, the bird also died.

You remember that there is a picture in which Napoleon is represented as riding over the battlefield, and he stopped his horse as he saw a slain man with his favorite dog lying upon his chest to do what he could to defend his dead master. Even the great manslayer paused at such a sight.

There is gratitude among the beasts of the field and the fowls of the air. And surely if we receive blessings from God without feeling love for Him in return, we are worse than brute beasts. Therefore the Lord, in that sad verse in Isaiah, pleads against us: *The ox knoweth his owner, and the ass his master's crib: but Israel doth not know, my people doth not consider* (Isaiah 1:3). If we receive favors from God, it is only natural that we should return them.

Gratitude, cheerful: I have sometimes admired a dog for his thrifty use of comforts. When it has been a long rainy day, the sun has just popped out, and there has been a gleam of sunlight on the floor, I have seen him get up, wag his tail, and crawl over so as to lie down where the bit of sunshine was. It is a fine thing to have just that state of mind never to go drearily into the shadow, but to always go cheerfully to accept the square foot of sunshine and make the most of it. There is something, after all, to be thankful for – something for which to praise the name of God.

Gratitude in heaven: I sometimes tell the story of what happened to me when I declared in a sermon that, in the heaven of the grateful, I would sing the loudest of them all because I owed more to the grace of God than anybody else. I did not mean it out of any sense of superiority, but rather inferiority. When I came down from the pulpit, one good old soul said to me, "You have made a great mistake in your sermon."

I answered, "No doubt I made a dozen."

"No," she said, "but the great mistake was this: you said you owed more to God than anybody else, but you do not owe anything like so much as I do. I have had more grace from Him than you have. I have been a bigger sinner than ever you were. I will sing the loudest."

"Well, well," I thought, "I will not quarrel with her; it will make me the more glad to find I am outdone."

I found that all the Christians were much of the same mind. Brethren, we will have it out when we get up there in heaven, but you will praise God indeed if you praise Him more than I will, and you must be double debtors to the Lord if you owe Him more than I do.

Greed of gain: I have distinctly seen a man become "the architect of his own fortune"[4] and the destroyer of himself. He has built up a palatial estate upon the ruins of his own manhood. It is a pity when a man bricks himself up with his growing gains. Do you see that hole in the wall? The man stands in it and greedily cries for bricks and mortar. He must have golden bricks and silver mortar. They bring him the materials. He cries eagerly for more. He cannot be content until he builds himself in. The wall that shuts him out from his fellow men and from the light of peace and true joy rises higher and higher, month by month and year by year. His sympathies and charities are bricked up, for the wall is more than chest high. Still he calls for more metallic material. At last he is built in, buried beneath his own gatherings, lost to all manhood through his accumulations.

You see his house, you see his carriages and his horses, and you see his fine clothes and his many acres – but you cannot see the man. Heart, soul, ambition, spirituality – it is all gone, and nothing remains except a vault of greed and care, to be itself buried beneath a monument bearing these words: "He died worth half a million."

Growth in grace: At first, we give little children types of food that will be easily absorbed. They have nothing but milk. Eventually, hard crusts are given to them, for there are teeth to be cut. Suppose when we give them more solid food, they began crying out for the milk again; should we give it

---

4   This is a quote by the Roman statesman Appius Claudius Caecus.

to them? The Lord does not want you to always be infants. He desires you to grow into men in Christ Jesus; and although Christ is always your food whether He comes to you as milk or as meat, yet still He will not always be milk to you so that you do not always remain as an infant. He intends to be meat to you so your senses may be exercised and so you may be able to understand the stronger and deeper truths of the kingdom of God.

Growth in grace: I have had the portraits of my two boys taken on their birthdays from their first birthday until they were twenty-one. The first year the little fellows are sitting, two of them in one baby carriage. At twenty-one, they are doing nothing of the sort. They are full-grown men. Yet I can trace them all along, from the time when they were babies until they became little boys, and then youths and young men. I would not have been pleased to have seen them wheeled around in the baby carriage for twenty-one years. In the same way, I do not want to have any of you remaining in spiritual infancy. We desire to see you come to the fullness of the stature of mature men in Christ Jesus (Ephesians 4:13).

Growth in grace: The other day there landed on the shores of France a boatful of people drenched with rain and saltwater. They had lost all their luggage and had nothing except what they stood upright in. They were glad, indeed, to have been saved from a wreck. It was good that they landed safely on shore at all. However, when I happen to cross to France again, I trust I will put my foot on shore in a better situation than that. I would prefer to cross the English Channel in comfort and land with pleasure.

There is all this difference between being saved *so as by fire* (1 Corinthians 3:15) and having an abundant entrance ministered unto us into the kingdom (2 Peter 1:11). Let us enjoy heaven on the road to heaven. Why not? Instead of being fished up as castaways, stranded upon the shores of mercy, let us take our passage on board the well-appointed liner of *Free Grace*. If possible, let us go in the first cabin, enjoying all the comforts of the way and having fellowship with the great Captain of our Salvation. Why would we think it is enough to be mere stowaways?

I would stir you up at this time, dear friends, to desire and pursue the best gifts. Grow in grace. Increase in love to God and in nearness of access to Him so that the Lord may at this good hour stoop down to us as our great Friend, and then lift us up to be known as His friends.

Growth in grace: Every man among us has to wear out at least one pair of green slippers, and after he has worn them out, he puts on something better by way of traveling gear and has his feet *shod with the preparation of the gospel of peace* (Ephesians 6:15). We generally begin with a fool's boots, but God, who makes the foolish wise, eventually makes men of us.

Growth in grace: Most of us remember our childish joy when we began to wear clothing that we thought would make us look like men. When I first wore boots and walked through the fields with my big uncle, I felt that I was somebody. That, of course, was childish pride, but it has its commendable analogy in the pleasure of gathering spiritual strength and becoming equal to higher labors and deeper experiences. When you find that you do not lose your temper under provocation as you did a year ago, you are humbly thankful. When an evil lust is driven away and no longer troubles you, you are quietly joyful, rejoicing with trembling. When you have sustained a trial that once would have crushed you, the victory is exceedingly sweet. Every advance in holiness is an advance in secret happiness.

Guidance, divine: There is a story told of a certain friend who one night was influenced to take his horse from the stable and ride some six or seven miles to a certain house where lived a person whom he had never seen. He arrived at the dead of night, knocked at the door, and was answered by the master of the house, who seemed to be in great confusion of mind. The midnight visitor said, "Friend, I have been sent to you. I do not know why, but the Lord certainly has some reason for having sent me to you. Is there anything unusual about your circumstances?"

The man, struck with amazement, asked him to come upstairs, where he showed him a rope tied to a beam. He was putting the rope around his neck to commit suicide when he heard a knock at the door. He decided to go down and answer the call and then return to destroy himself, but the friend whom God had sent talked to him and helped him, and the man lived to be an honorable Christian man.

* * * *

- Get right within, and you will be right without.

- God blesses us many times every time He blesses us.

- God can use inferior people for great purposes.

- God gives small creatures great delight.

- God has no thunderbolts for those who hate their sins.

- Godliness is not a torture rack nor a thumbscrew.

- Godly people are thoughtful people. Indeed, it is often a sign of the beginning of grace in a man when he begins to consider.

- Good delayed is evil indulged.

- Good works are not to be an amusement, but a life's work.

- Grace baptizes us into blessedness.

- Grace does not exempt us from activity.

- Grace makes the servant of God to be in the highest sense a true gentleman.

- Grace personally received must be personally acknowledged.

- Great birds seldom have the gift of song.

- Grief has little regard for the laws of the grammarian.

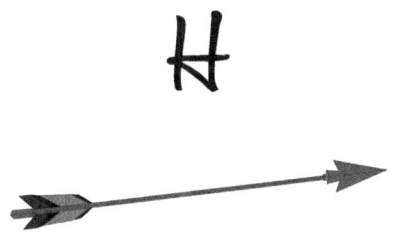

Happy dying: Mr. Rowland Hill used to merrily say when he got old that he hoped they had not forgotten him.[5] That is how he came to look at death. He would go to some old woman if he could, and say, "Now, dear sister, if you go before I go, be sure to give my love to John Bunyan and the other Johns. Tell them that Rowley is stopping behind a little while, but he is coming on as fast as he can." Oh, it is a sweet thing to gradually melt away and have the tenement gradually taken down, and yet not to feel any trouble about it, but to know that you are in the great Father's hands and you will wake up where old age and infirmities will all have passed away, and where, in everlasting youth, you will behold the face of Him you love.

Hard to die: A wise man said to a worldly person, when he looked over his beautiful gardens, "These are the things that make it hard to die. You will have to leave everything that you call your own here, and you have no possessions over there."

Hearers, forgetful: There is a sad tendency in many hearers to forget the essential point and think of our stories and illustrations rather than of the practical duty that we want to emphasize. A celebrated minister, who has long ago gone home, was once taken ill, and his wife requested him to go and consult an eminent physician. He went to this physician,

---

5   A biography of Rowland Hill (which contains an introduction by Charles Spurgeon) is available from Aneko Press.

who welcomed him very warmly. "I am very glad to see you, sir," he said. "I have heard you preach and have been greatly profited by you, and therefore I have often wanted to have half an hour's chat with you. If I can do anything for you, I certainly will."

The minister stated his case. The doctor said, "Oh, it is a very simple matter. You only have to take such and such a drug, and you will soon be all right."

The patient was about to go, thinking that he must not take up too much of the physician's time, but the physician urged him to stay, and they entered into a pleasant conversation. The minister went home to his wife and told her with joy what a delightful man the doctor had proved to be. He said, "I do not know that I ever had a more delightful talk. The good man is eloquent, witty, and gracious."

The wife replied, "But what remedy did he prescribe?"

"Dear," said the minister, "I completely forgot what he told me about that."

She said, "What? Did you go to a physician for advice, and have you come away without a remedy?"

"It completely slipped my mind," he said. "The doctor talked so pleasantly that his prescription has quite gone out of my head."

Don't be a forgetful hearer.

Heart, an evil: Pliny was accustomed to say that it was a miracle that the world escaped burning for a single day, and I do not wonder at the remark, considering the character of the district in which he spent much of his time. Near him was Vesuvius, ready at any moment to vomit fire, and continually sending up clouds of smoke. Ascend the mountainside, stumbling over ashes and masses of lava. Everything beneath you is glowing. Thrust in your staff, and it is charred.

Heart, lost: I knew a man who lost his heart. His wife did not have it, and his children did not have it, and he did not seem as if he himself had it. "That is odd," you say. Well, he used to starve himself. He hardly had enough to eat. His clothes were threadbare. He starved all who were around him. He did not seem to have a heart. A poor woman owed him a little rent. Out she went into the street. He had no heart.

A person had fallen back a little in the payment of money that he had lent him. The debtor's little children were crying for bread. The man did not care who cried for hunger or what became of the children. He wanted his money. He had lost his heart.

I never could figure out where it was until I went to his house one day and I saw a huge chest. I think they called it an iron safe. It stood behind the door of an inner room. When he unlocked it with a heavy key, when the bolts were slid over, and when the inside was opened, there was a musty, decaying thing within it, as dry and dead as the kernel of a walnut seven years old. It was his heart.

If you have locked up your heart in an iron safe, get it out as quickly as you can. It is a horrible thing to pack up a heart in dollar bills or to bury it under piles of silver and gold. Hearts are never healthy when covered up with hard metal. Your gold and silver are polluted if your heart is bound up with them.

Heart, will of God in the: I heard of a famous king of Poland who did brave deeds in his day, and he confessed that he owed his excellent character to a secret habit he had formed. He was the son of a noble father, and he carried with him a miniature portrait of this father that he often looked at. Whenever he went to battle, he would look at the picture of his father and strengthen himself for battle. When he sat in the council chamber, he would secretly look upon the image of his father and would conduct himself right royally, for he said, "I will do nothing that can dishonor my father's name." This is a very important thing for a Christian to do – to carry about with him the will of God in his heart, and then in every action to consult that will.

Heavenly choir: The music of the heavenly harmonies as yet lacks certain voices. Some of its needful notes are too low for those already there, and others are too high for them, until the singers come who are ordained to give the choir its fullest range. At a concert, you have seen the singers marching in. The conductor is full of anxiety if they seem to linger. Still, some are away. The time is nearly up, and you see seats up there on the right and an empty section down there on the left. That is how it is with the heavenly choir. They are streaming in and the orchestra is filling up, but there is still room, and there is still demand for other voices to complete the heavenly harmony.

Heaven, going to: It is not worthwhile going to heaven alone. A little lost child sits down on the doorstep of a mansion and cries because he is so lonely. Is that to be our position in heaven? Are we not going to take any friends there with us? Who wants to be alone in the new Jerusalem?

Heaven in us: An old Scotchman was asked whether he expected to get to heaven. "Why, man, I live there," was his quaint reply. Let us all live in those spiritual things that are the essential features of heaven. Go there often before you go to stay there. It was said of Richard Sibbes, an old Puritan, that heaven was in him before he was in heaven. That is necessary for all of us. We must have heaven in us before we get into heaven. If we do not get to heaven before we die, we will never get there afterward.

Heaven, near: The other day I saw the white cliffs of Dover. The swift ship had performed the passage so rapidly that the sea had been crossed before I had figured on reaching land. There were the cliffs just ahead. Brethren, heaven is just ahead! Run to the bows! Heaven ahoy! Do not forever continue gazing at the misty shores behind you. Look ahead! You are far nearer than you think to the land of the immortal! We are within speaking distance of heaven! The Lord hears our cry, and we hear His promise.

> How near to faith's far-seeing eye
> The golden gates appear![6]

Heaven or hell our port: If I were to go out tomorrow by sea, I would not walk on board a steamer and then ask, "Where are you going?" I first make up my mind where I will go, and then I select a vessel that is likely to take me there in comfort. You must know where you are going. The main thing with the captain of a ship will be getting his vessel safely into the port for which it is bound. This desire overrules everything

---

6   This is from a hymn by James Montgomery (1771-1854) that begins with "Forever with the Lord!"

else. To get into port is the thought of every watch, every glance at the chart, and every observation of the stars. The captain's heart is set upon the other side. His hope is to safely arrive at the desired haven, and he knows which is the haven of his choice. He would not expect to get there if he did not set his mind on it. How is it with you, dear friend? You are speeding toward heaven or hell: which of these is your port?

Holiday Christians: "Is your father a Christian?" asked a Sunday school teacher to a child. The girl answered, "Yes, I believe that Father is a Christian, but he has not worked much at it lately." No doubt there are many people like that. Their religion has taken a vacation, and they themselves have gone to a sluggard's bed. Let them be awakened, for *it is high time to awake out of sleep* (Romans 13:11).

Holy bravery: A person under the influence of alcohol will do what he would never think of doing at any other time. He will be reckless, foolish, and daring to the last degree. We have heard of foreign nations whose troops have been so afraid of the fight that they have given them strong drink to induce them to march into battle. We used to hear the expression, "Dutch courage," which meant the boldness that came from ardent spirits – though I do not suppose the Dutch had more of it than the English.

No doubt many people under the influence of alcohol have risked their lives and performed what look like feats of valor, when indeed they were simply beyond themselves and out of their right minds, or they would not have been so foolhardy. Wine emboldens many people in the wrong way. Beloved friends, we are not to make ourselves foolish with fanaticism, but bold with the Spirit of truth. *Be not drunk with wine, wherein is excess,* in order to gain motivation to do anything, but *be filled with the Spirit* of the living God (Ephesians 5:18), wherein is quietness, and from whom comes a courage that is to be admired and not ridiculed. Oh, how brave a man is when he is filled with the Spirit of God!

Holy Spirit, pray for the: Sometimes when we are praying that we may feel the power of the Word, we hardly know what we are praying for. I saw an honorable brother the other day, and he said to me, "I remember speaking with you when you were nineteen or twenty years of age, and I never forgot what you said to me. I had been praying with you in the prayer meeting that God would give us the Holy Spirit to the full, and you said to me afterward, 'My dear brother, do you know what you asked God for?' I answered, 'Yes.' But you very solemnly said to me, 'The Holy Spirit is the Spirit of judgment and the Spirit of burning, and few are prepared for the inward conflict that is meant by these two words.'"

My good old friend told me that at the time he did not understand what I meant, but thought of me as a strange youth. "Ah!" he said, "I see it now, but it is only by a painful experience that I have come to fully understand it."

Yes, for when Christ comes, He comes not to send peace on the earth, but a sword (Matthew 10:34), and that sword begins at home in our own souls, killing, cutting, hacking, and breaking in pieces. Blessed is that man who knows the Word of the Lord by its exceeding sharpness, for it kills nothing except that which should be killed.

Holy Spirit like the wind: In this land especially, we can never tell what wind will blow tomorrow. A few days ago it was the southwest wind, and it brought a rapid thaw, but the next morning it was nearly north, and a frost was upon us. We may well put vanes on our public buildings, for without them we could never tell from the day or season of the year from what direction the wind would come. I feel thankful when I remember that, like the wind, the Holy Spirit blows where He desires (John 3:8), for I cannot tell where He may operate next.

Holy Spirit our guide: The truth is something like those stalactite caverns and caves that you must enter and see for yourself if you really want to know their wonders. If you should venture there without light or guide, you would run great risks, but with blazing torches and an instructed leader, your entrance is full of interest. See, your guide has taken you through a narrow, winding passage where you have to crawl or go on bended knees. At last he has brought you into a magnificent hall, and when the torches are held high, the far-off roof sparkles and flashes back the light as from countless jewels of every hue. You now behold nature's architecture, and cathedrals are from now on as toys to you. As you stand in that vast pillared and jeweled palace, you feel how much you owe to your guide and to his flaming torch. Thus the Holy Spirit leads us into all truth and sheds light on the eternal and the mysterious.

"Honest doubt": Unbelief calls itself "honest doubt," and not without cause, for we would not have known it to be honest if it had not labeled itself so. When a man puts up in his shop window, "No cheating practiced here," I would do business next door. He doth protest too much.[7] Your free love, free thought, free life, and so forth are the empty mockery of freedom.

Honest failure: A good doctor of divinity met a Christian man in the street, shook hands with him, and congratulated him. The man said, "I do not know why you would congratulate me, for I have had a world of trouble; in fact, I have failed in my business."

The doctor replied, "I congratulate you because you failed honestly. You are the only man for years I have seen fail like that." Then he shook hands with him again, and said, "My dear fellow, I do thank God you failed honestly." No one fails if he serves God.

Honesty needs no defense: The Chinese trader who put over his shops, "No cheating here," turned out to be the biggest cheat in the street. If you are honest, you will confess that you have sinned, and then you will come to Jesus for that remission of sins that comes through His sacrifice.

Hope, a cheerless: When I was in the Church of St. John Lateran at Rome, I read a request for prayer for the rest of the soul of his Eminence, Cardinal Wiseman. Cardinal Wiseman was a great man, a prince of the Roman Catholic Church, yet he is somewhere in the other world where he is not in rest; so this request indicates. If this is true of Cardinal Wiseman, there must be a very poor outlook for an ordinary Catholic. For my part, I would give up such a cheerless hope and become a believer in the Lord Jesus Christ and go to heaven.

---

7   "The lady doth protest too much, methinks" is a line from William Shakespeare's play *Hamlet*.

Hope for great sinners: You remember what the Scottish woman said to Rowland Hill when she stood looking at his face. He said, "Well, good woman, you have looked at me a long while. What are you looking at?"

She said, "I was looking at the lines of your face."

"Well, what do you make of them?" he said.

"I was thinking what a terrible reprobate you would have been if you were not converted," was her unexpected answer.

Now I think we could say the same about a good many people, and if it is God's intent, He would get a glorious name for Himself. I see hope for big reprobates. I see hope for great sinners.

Human efforts are vain: Human effort and self-righteousness are like a man trying to patch up an old house. You find such homes in country villages – places that nobody has repaired for fifty years. I do not know if there is any landlord, but if there is, he would like to forget that he has such property. The main beam is nearly cracked through. The lath and plaster have gone long ago, and the birds go in and out the best room whenever they like. The whole thing is tumbling down. A man buys it, and he says, "Now, you know, it is a pity to pull this house down. I think I will repair it." So he puts in a beam there, just under the roof, and he puts a strut here and another timber there, and by the time he has spent as much as he would have if he had built a house, he has got a very nice-looking ruin left, and nothing more.

Human instrumentality: I read the other day of a certain writer who said, "I wrote all four hundred pages of this book with one pen." Where is that pen? Does anybody want it? If it were advertised as an exhibition, I would not go to see it. I care much more for the hand that wrote, and for what was written, than for the pen with which it was written. It was a common goose quill in the case referred to, and nothing more. Oh, how plainly we can see where the quill came from! God uses people for a certain purpose, just as we use a hammer, or a saw, or a drill.

Suppose that when we were finished with such tools, and had put them away, they all began to cry, "See what we have done! What a sharp saw I was! What a heavy hammer I was! Did I not hit the nail on the head?" Such boastings would be foolishness. *Shall the axe boast itself against him that heweth therewith?* (Isaiah 10:15). We do not think that the instrument should take credit for itself, but it does so in our case whenever it can, and this is a great detriment to us. Some of us could have enjoyed a much larger blessing if we had not grown top heavy with the blessing we already enjoyed.

Hunger belt: When the poor Bushmen have nothing to eat, they tie a girdle around them and call it the hunger belt, and when they have gone a few days, they pull it tighter still, and tighter still, in order to enable them to bear hunger. In the same way, any man who has to live upon himself will have to draw the hunger belt very tight indeed. A soul cannot be persuaded by philosophy to be content without its necessary food. Eloquence may try all its charms to that end, but it will be in vain.

Hunger, best appetite: The person who has grown accustomed to luxuries is the person who turns his meat over and picks off a bit here and a bit there, for this is too fat, and that is too gristly. Bring in the poor wretches who are half-starved. Bring in a group of laborers who have been waiting all day at the docks and have found no work, and in consequence have received no wage. Set them down to a piece of meat. It vanishes before them. See what masters they are of the art of knife and fork! They find no fault. They never dream of such a thing. If the meat is a little coarse, it does not matter to them; their need is too great for them to be dainty. Oh, for a host of hungry souls! How pleasant to feed them! How different from the task of persuading the overfed Pharisees to partake of the gospel!

Hunger deadened: I am told that there is a country (I think it is Patagonia) where men in times of hunger eat clay in great lumps and fill themselves with it so as to deaden their hunger. I know that many people in England do the same. There is a kind of yellow clay that is much recommended for repressing spiritual hunger. It is heavy stuff, but many have a vast appetite for it. They prefer it to the finest foods.

Hypocrites: We cannot prevent hypocrites from arising. It is only proof that true religion is worth having. You were given a counterfeit twenty-dollar bill the other night. Did you say, "All twenty-dollar bills are worthless. I will never accept another one"? No. You became more careful, but you were quite sure there were good twenty-dollar bills in circulation, or else people would not make counterfeit ones. It would not benefit anybody to be a hypocrite unless there were enough genuine Christians to make the hypocrites seem real.

* * * *

- Halfway-house godliness is horrible stuff.
- Hannibal, it is said, dissolved the rocks of the Alps with vinegar; but Christ dissolves our hearts with love.
- Have the blood-mark very visible on all your mercies.
- Heaven hides itself away within the gospel.
- He who can stand on the hilltop can stand in the valley.
- He wears for His princely star the lance mark in His side.
- Holiness is the royal road to scriptural knowledge.
- How can a soul make progress if it is always changing its course? Do not sow in Beersheba and then rush off to reap in Dan.

I

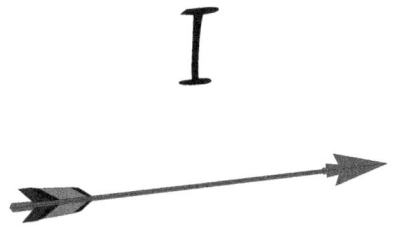

"If" of doubt removed: I heard of a little girl whose mother found her one day with a carving knife and the family Bible. "What are you doing?" she asked, in some surprise, for the safety of both Bible and child.

"Oh, Mother," she said, "I was reading about the man who came to Jesus and said, 'If thou wilt, thou canst make me clean'; and I thought he should not have said 'if' to Jesus; so please, mother, I am scraping it out." That is a very good thing to do with all our "ifs."

Ill-feeling cured by kindness: Yesterday I heard of a wise old Welsh minister of a generous spirit who was afflicted with a horrible deacon. If a deacon is unkind, he can wound terribly. This deacon was most perverse and cruel, and tormented the old gentleman in all sorts of ways. Eventually he became sick, after having said certain dreadful things that were more bitter than even his usual gall and wormwood. The patient pastor soon went to see him, and on the road he bought some of the best oranges and took them with him. "Brother Jones," he said, "I am sorry you are so ill. I have come to see you, and I have brought you a few oranges."

Brother Jones was very much astonished at this kind act and did not have much to say on the matter. The minister gently continued, saying, "I think it would refresh you to eat one of these. I will peel you one." So he peeled the orange and talked with him pleasantly. Then he divided the fruit very neatly and handed the sick man a nice piece in the gentlest possible manner. The bitter-spirited man ate it and began to melt a little. The conversation became friendly, and the prayer was pleasant. Brother Jones was getting better in more ways than one.

An outsider, who knew all about Brother Jones and his disagreeableness, could hardly believe that the minister had acted in such a way to one who had opposed him constantly and slandered him so terribly, and so he asked, "Did you really go and see that cruel old Jones?"

"Oh, yes," he said, "I went to see him. It was my duty to do so."

"And did you take him some oranges?"

"Oh, yes, I took him some oranges. I was glad to do so."

"And did you sit down by his bedside and peel him an orange?"

"Yes, I peeled him an orange, and I was pleased to see him enjoy it; for I have learned, brother, that when a man is afflicted with a very bad temper, an orange is a good thing for him to take. At any rate, it is a good thing for one to give."

The lesson is that if you want to cure a man of his disagreeableness, be very kind to him. View unkind and bad-tempered speeches as symptoms of a disease for which the best medicine is not a dose of bitter medicine, but an orange.

Imagination, vain: I have heard a story that the Chinese sell shoes with which you can walk on the clouds. I believe that some people must have bought a pair of these remarkable articles, for their lives are spent in cloudland, walking as in a dream upon high stilts of fond imagination. Do not think great things of yourself. You are but a commonplace man or woman.

Imperfection, unacceptable: Here is a chain containing twenty links. If I break one of them, I have broken the chain. It is true that there are nineteen perfect links, but if number twenty is snapped, down goes the cage over the mouth of the mine, and the miners are killed. Suppose that I would be required to produce a perfect vase of alabaster or clear crystal as a present to the queen, but my maid servant has chipped it a little. What is to be done? I may possibly find somebody to use some patent cement and fasten the little pieces in their places, but when all is done, it is chipped. It is not perfect, and if it must be perfect before royalty can accept it, I must get another vase, for this one will not do.

Importunity in prayer: I do not suppose any of you desire a beggar to continue to bother you. Did you ever say, "Whenever I go across this crossing, ask me for some money. If I do not give you any, ask me, run after me, and call after me all the way down the street. If that does not work, lay hold upon me until I help you. Beg without ceasing." Did any of you ever invite applicants to call often and make large requests of you? Oh, no. Importunity is a common enough thing when people are seeking earthly benefits, but it is so sadly rare in heavenly concerns that the Lord has to exhort us to be importunate with Him. He does basically say, "Call upon Me. Urge Me. Lay hold on My strength. Wrestle with Me as when a man seeks to give another a fall so that he may prevail with him."

Inferior pursuits: I met with a clergyman many years ago who was going a long distance to find a new beetle. He was a great entomologist, and I did not blame him for it, for to a thoughtful man, entomology may yield many profitable lessons. But if he neglected his preaching to catch insects, then I do not wonder that a parishioner would wish that the beetles would nibble his old sermons, for they were very stale. I call it choking the seed when any inferior pursuit becomes the master of our minds and the cause of God and truth takes a secondary place.

Influence, power of godly: I remember hearing Mr. Jay tell a story about a Nonconformist servant girl who went to live in a family of worldly people who attended the Church of England, although they were not real believers. They supported the Church from the outside, but they had very little to do with the inside of it – and outsiders are generally the most bigoted. They were very angry with their servant for going to the little meetinghouse to hear the Nonconformist preacher, and they threatened to discharge her if she went again. But she went again all the same and very kindly but firmly assured them that she must go again. At last she received notice that she should find a different place of employment, for as good Church of England people, they could not have a Dissenter living with them.

She took their rough dismission very patiently, and it came to pass that the day before she was to leave, a conversation of this sort took place.

Her master said, "It is a pity, after all, that Jane should go. We never had such a good employee. She is very industrious, truthful, and attentive."

The wife said, "Well, I have thought it is hardly right to send her away for going to her chapel. You always speak up for religious liberty, and it does not quite look like religious liberty to turn our girl away for worshiping God according to her conscience. I am sure she is much more careful about religion than we are."

So they talked it over and said, "She has never answered us rudely or found fault about our going to our church. Her religion is a greater comfort to her than ours is to us. We had better let her stay with us and let her go where she likes."

"Yes," said the husband, "and I think we had better go and hear the minister she hears. Evidently she has got something we have not. Instead of sending her away, we will go with her to hear for ourselves."

And they did, and it was not long before the master and mistress were members of that church.

Inner light: A clean lantern with a lit candle makes no noise, yet it wins attention. The darker the night, the more it is valued. There never was a time when true inner light was more needed than now. May the Lord impart it to each one of us, and then we will shine as lights in the world.

Insensibility to death: In the higher and colder latitudes, when men feel a sleepiness coming over them, their companions stir them up, have them move around, and will not let them slumber; for to sleep is to wake no more. The man pleads, "Let me sleep for half an hour, and I will be so refreshed." Alas! If he sleeps, he will not do well, for he will grow rigid in the death that frost brings to him. Go on, wise friends, and compassionately shake him! Hurry him to and fro, or shake him vigorously until he grows sore. I cannot get hold of you at this present hour with my hands, nor would I want to give you a bodily shaking – but oh, that I could do this spiritually and wake you up! I cannot leave you to sleep your soul into hell.

Introspection: Some people spend much of their time in what is called introspection. Introspection, like retrospection, is a useful thing in part, but it can easily be overdone, and then it breeds dreary emotions and creates despair. Some people are always looking into their own feelings. A healthy man hardly knows whether he has a stomach or a liver. It is the one is sick who grows more sickly by studying his inward complaints.

Too many people wound themselves by studying themselves. Every morning they think of what they should feel. All day long they dwell upon what they are not feeling. At night they make diligent search for what they have been feeling. It looks to me like shutting up your shop and then living in the warehouse, thinking about what is not sold. Small profits will be made in this way. You may look a long while into an empty pocket before you find a coin, and you may look a long time into fallen nature before you find comfort.

A person might as well try to find burning coals under the ice as to find anything good in our poor human nature. When you look within, it should be to see with grief what the filthiness is; but to get rid of that filthiness, you must look beyond yourself. I remember Mr. Moody saying that a mirror was a great thing to show you the spots on your face, but you could not wash in a mirror. You need something very different when you want to make your face clean.

Inward piety: A form of godliness joined to an unholy heart is of no value to God. I have read that the swan was not allowed to be offered upon the altar of God because, although its feathers are as white as snow, yet its skin is not. God will not accept that external morality that conceals internal impurity. There must be a pure heart as well as a clean life. The power of godliness must work within, or else God will not accept our offering. There is no value to man or to God in a religion that is a dead form.

* * * *

- Idle words are in the speech of man, not in the writings of Jehovah.

- I do not believe in an atonement that is admirably wide, but fatally powerless.

- If the devil never roars, the church will never sing.

- If we do not praise Him, we deserve to be banished to the Siberia of despair.

- If we were a little slower, we would be quicker.

- If your life pleases God, let it please you.

- I have heard of Latter-day Saints; I far more admire Every-day Saints.

- In a dewdrop, the sun may be reflected.

- It is always easy to rise up early during the night.

- It takes more grace to lead than to follow.

- I would rather obey God than rule an empire.

J

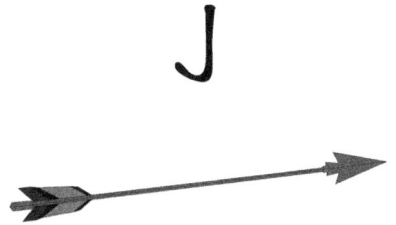

Jesus, a light: If I saw a man going into a school for the blind, and he was installing lights or running wires for light switches, I would feel certain that he was doing so for people who can see; and if no one except blind people could come into the building, I would conclude that he anticipated a time when the poor blind folks would find their sight again and would be able to use the light. In the same way, as the Lord has sent Jesus to be a light, you may be sure that He intends to open blind eyes. Jesus will enlighten the people and souls will be saved.

Jesus Himself: I see at times in the newspaper, "Main parties only will be dealt with," and in our heavenly business, we had better keep to this rule. Do not go to the servants. Make all your requests to the Master, and in your dealings with Him, do not seek His gifts as much as Himself, for the Giver is always greater than what He gives. The bottle of water that Hagar carried for Ishmael is a poor thing compared with that well of God beside which Isaac abode. Fruit from a healthy tree is good; apples of gold in baskets of silver are not to be despised – but if one can have the tree planted in his own garden, he is far richer.

Our Lord is the *apple tree among the trees of the wood* (Song of Solomon 2:3), and to possess Him is to have the best of the best – to have all things that can be desired. Covenant blessings are streams, but our Lord Jesus is the wellspring. Believe for the infinite, immutable, inexhaustible *deep that lieth under* (Genesis 49:25), and you may drill as many wells as you please.

Jesus, "Looking unto": I have read of a competition between certain young plowmen who were set to plow for a prize. Most of them made very crooked work of it. After they had finished, one of the judges said, "Young man, where did you look while you were plowing?"

"I kept my eyes well on the plow handles, sir, and saw what I had to hold."

"Yes," the judge said, "and your plow went in and out, and the furrow is all crooked."

He asked the next plowman, "And where did you look?"

"Well, sir," he answered, "I looked at my furrow. I kept my eye always on the furrow that I was making. I thought I would make it straight that way."

"But you did not," answered the judge, "you were all over the place."

To the next man he said, "What did you look at?"

"Well, sir," he said, "I looked between the two horses to a tree that stood in the hedge at the other end of the field, right in front of me."

That man went straight because he had a fixed mark to guide him. This helps us to appreciate the wisdom of the text, *Looking unto Jesus* (Hebrews 12:2). Run. Run straight. You cannot run straight unless you keep your eye on the One who is always the same. *Looking unto Jesus, the author and finisher of our faith*, is a sure way to keep you from wandering. Spiritual plowmen, take heed that you do not look back, but plow a straight furrow toward Jesus on the throne!

"Jesus, lover of my soul": I think I have read somewhere that one morning Charles Wesley was getting dressed. His window looked out toward the sea, and there was a heavy wind blowing. The waves were very boisterous, and the rain was falling heavily. Just then a little bird, overtaken by the storm, flew in at the open window and nestled in his arms. Of course, he cherished it there and then urged it to go on its way when the storm was over. Impressed by the interesting occurrence, he sat down and wrote the verse:

> Jesus, lover of my soul,
>> Let me to Thy bosom fly.
>> While the raging billows roll,

> While the tempest still is high.
> Hide me, O my Savior, hide,
>> Till the storm of life be past.
> Safe into the haven guide.
>> Oh, receive my soul at last.

Imitate that poor little bird if you want to have Christ. Fly away from the wrath of God, fly away from your own convictions of sin, fly away from your dark forebodings of judgment to come, right into the arms of Jesus, which are warm with love to sinners.

Jesus only: I remember a story told about William Dawson, whom our Wesleyan friends used to call Billy Dawson – one of the best preachers who ever entered a pulpit. He once gave out as his text, *Through this man is preached unto you the forgiveness of sins* (Acts 13:38). After he had given out his text, he dropped down to the bottom of the pulpit so that nothing could be seen of him. There was only a voice heard saying, "Not the man in the pulpit; he is out of sight, but the Man in the Book. The Man described in the Book is the Man through whom is preached unto you the remission of sins."

I put myself and you and everybody else out of sight, and I preach to you the remission of sins through Jesus only. I would sing with the children, "Nothing but the blood of Jesus." Shut your eyes to all things but the cross.

Jesus will win at last: I shook hands after one morning's sermon with a good missionary of Christ from West Africa. He had been there sixteen years. I believe that they consider four years to be the average missionary's life in that district that is full of malaria. He had buried twelve of his companions during his time there. For twelve years, he had scarcely seen the face of a white man. He was going to Africa to live a little while longer, perhaps, but he expected to die soon, and then he added (I thought, sweetly), as I shook his hand, "Well, many of us may die; perhaps hundreds of us will – but Christ will win at last. Africa will know and fear our Lord Jesus, and what does it matter what becomes of us – our name, our reputation, our life, our health – if Jesus wins at last." What heroic words! What a missionary spirit!

Joy rapturous through faith: John Bunyan pictures Christiana as saying to Mercy, "What was the reason that you laughed in your sleep last night?"

Mercy answered, "But are you sure I laughed?"

When she told her dream, Christiana said, "Laugh, yes; you might well laugh to see yourself so well."

She laughed because she dreamed that she had been welcomed into glory. To faith, this is no dream. We have had many dreams of this kind, and we know that we are saved by grace, adopted by the Father, united to the Son, and indwelt by the Holy Spirit – visions most true, and these have made us laugh with an inward inexpressible delight. The more steadfastly we believe, the more of this rapturous joy we will experience.

Judgments, national: National judgments are frequently a ministry of grace. The first year that I came to London, I was greatly amazed by the access that one had at all hours of the day and night to people's houses, into which no ministers of Christ had ever been welcomed before. At two o'clock one Monday morning I was in a house, close to London Bridge, to see a man who had spent the Sunday at Brighton and had come home to die with the cholera. Yes, they often sent for me in the middle of the night; and rich and poor – it mattered not, if they found someone willing to come and visit them – were eager for you to read and pray with them, for death was all around us making havoc in these streets. They are not so eager for a visit now. So far, cholera did awaken our neighbors, and they flocked to hear the Word out of very fear. There may be much benefit in the plagues that are shot from the quiver of Providence.

Just, yet merciful: Some time ago, a judge in America was called upon to try a prisoner who had been his companion in his early youth. It was a crime for which the penalty was a heavy fine. The judge did not diminish the fine. The case was clearly a bad one, and he fined the prisoner to the full. Someone who knew his former relation to the offender thought he had been somewhat unkind to carry out the law in this way, while others admired his impartiality.

All were surprised when the judge stepped down from the bench and paid every penny of the penalty himself. He had shown both his respect for the law and his goodwill to the man who had broken it. He enacted the penalty, but he paid it himself. This is what God has done in the person of His dear Son. He has not decreased or set aside the punishment, but He has Himself endured it. His own Son, who is none other than God Himself – for there is an essential union between them – has paid the debt that was incurred by human sin.

* * * *

- **Jesus** will never be a part Savior.

K

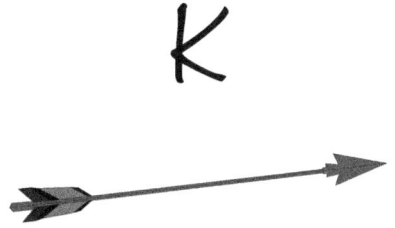

Kicking Christians: The driver of a bus was using his whip pretty freely on one of his horses, and a gentleman on the box seat observed that he never struck the other one. "Bless you, sir, if I was to touch that mare, she would kick me like a Christian when I went near her in the stable at night." What a remarkable simile, was it not? "Like a Christian." Is that so – that Christians kick, that they are found taking revenge? This is a matter about which we would urgently cry, *Be ye not as the horse, or as the mule* (Psalm 32:9). Never render *evil for evil, or railing for railing* (1 Peter 3:9), for that is to copy the beasts of the field.

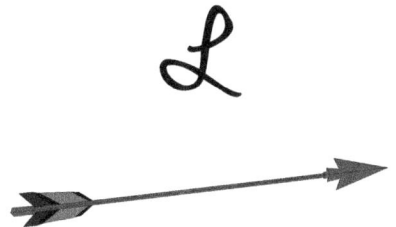

Laborers are few: Let me tell you what you are like. It is a hot autumn day, and a man is reaping. The sweat pours from his face as he bends to the task, and he fears that he will never get to the end of the field. All the time you are pleasantly occupied leaning over a gate, saying, "That is an exceptionally good laborer." Or perhaps instead of doing that, you are saying, "Why does he not handle the sickle properly? I could show him a better way of reaping." But since you never attempt to show him, we only have your own word to go by, and you must excuse us for being a little skeptical on the matter. The work of the church is generally left to a few earnest people, is it not? Is that right?

Liberty from death: The Roman emperor Theodosius, in a burst of a great good mood, set at liberty all people in prison or in captivity. Then he sighed and wished he could release the dead from their graves. Theodosius could not reach the key to the graves, for these hang from the belt of the Prince of Life. When He returns, He will open the iron gates and will tell the multitudes to pour forth as bees from a hive.

Liberty to captive souls: A sailor who had long been a prisoner in France gained his liberty. He went into the shopping district of Seven Dials, bought a cage full of birds, opened the cage, and let the birds fly. People cried with wonder, "What did you buy them for?"

"Oh! I bought them to let them fly. I know what it is to be a prisoner myself, and I cannot stand to see birds shut up in a cage." Go to those who are what you were – caged birds – and let them fly by telling them of Jesus and of the ransom price. Seek out poor, bound sinners, and proclaim freedom to them. Proclaim liberty at the market cross in the name of Christ.

Life is a mighty thing: Life is full of power. I have seen an iron bar bent by the growth of a tree. Have you never heard of great paving stones being lifted by fungi that had pushed up beneath them? Life, especially divine life, is a mighty thing. If you choose to contract your soul by a sport of spiritual tightlacing,[8] or if you choose to bend yourself down in a sorrow that never looks up, you may hinder your life and its walk. However, if you give your life full scope, what a walk you may have! Yield yourselves fully to God, and you will see what you will see. There is a happiness to be enjoyed by truly wholehearted believers that some, even of God's own children, would think to be impossible.

Life, its uncertainty: There are ten thousand gates to death. One man is choked by a grape. Another dies through sleeping in a newly white-washed room. Someone else receives death as he passes by a reeking sewer. Another person finds death in the best-kept house or by a chill taken in a walk. Those who study neither to eat nor to drink anything unhealthy, nor go into areas where the arrows of death are flying, still pass away suddenly, falling from their couch into a coffin, from their seat into the sepulcher. The other day, one of our own brethren sat down in his chair to sleep for a moment, but it was his last sleep. Another man stumbled in his own room never again to rise. These men were apparently in good health. Life is never certain for even an instant.

Light in the heart: Some people who profess to be Christian appear to have a little light in the upper rooms; they have opinions in their heads and ideas on their tongues. Sadly, the first floor is dark, very dark. Based upon their common conversation, the light of God is absent. Enter at the door, and you cannot see your way into the hallway or up the stairs. The light is on upstairs, but not in the living rooms. Oh, for a light in the region of the heart! Oh, for a light upon the household talk and the

---

8   Tightlacing was the practice of wearing a tightly laced corset.

business conversation! From attic to cellar, may the whole houses of our humanity be lit up. The true work of grace is when the whole man is brought into the light, and no part is left to languish in the darkness. Then are we the children of light – when we abide in the light and have no fellowship with darkness (Ephesians 5:8, 11).

Light, our joy: A poor boy who was put down in the coal mines to close a door after the coal wagons had passed by was forced to sit there alone, hour after hour, in the dark. He was a gracious child, and when someone said to him, "Are you not weary with sitting so long in the dark?" he said, "Yes, I do get tired; but sometimes the men give me a bit of candle, and when I get a light, I sing." So do we; when we get a light, we sing. Glory be to God! He is our light and our salvation, and therefore we sing. O child of God, when your eye is single (Matthew 6:22), and the light of God fills every part of your being, then you sing, and sing again, and feel that you can never be finished singing on earth until you begin singing in heaven.

Little faith: God deals with little faith as we used to do with a spark in the tinder in the days of our boyhood. When we had struck a spark and it fell into the tinder – even though it was a very tiny one – we watched it eagerly, we blew upon it softly, and we were zealous to increase it so that we might kindle our match by it. When our Lord Jesus sees a tiny spark of faith in a person's heart, even though it is quite insufficient of itself for salvation, yet He regards it with hope and watches over it in case this little faith grows to something more. It is the way of our compassionate Lord not to quench the smoking flax nor break the bruised reed (Isaiah 42:3).

Living, a plan of: A philosopher has remarked that if a man knew that he had thirty years of life before him, it would not be an unwise thing to spend twenty of those in mapping out a plan of living and putting himself under rule; for he would do more with the ten well-arranged years than with the whole thirty if he spent them at random. There is much truth in that saying. A man will not do much good by firing off his gun if he has not learned to take aim.

Locality, good: I know a brother who wanted to buy a certain shop in a wide street, but his wiser friends said, "Do not use that shop for a baker's. It is not in a good eating locality. You must open a shop in one of the streets where there are plenty of poor people who will buy the bread every morning. Make it good and cheap, and the bread will not be on the shelves for long." I noticed in the newspaper that a certain drink shop was "in a good drinking locality." I am sorry that there are such localities. But assuredly, a good eating locality must be the very place for selling bread.

Looking gives a claim: I remind you of what the little boys sometimes do at school with one another. I have seen a boy take an apple out of his pocket and say to his schoolmate, "Do you see that apple?"

"Yes," says his mate.

"Then see me eat it," he says.

But the Holy Spirit is not something always out of reach, taking the things of Christ and holding them up to mock us. No. Rather, He says, "Do you see those things? If so, you can have them." Did not Christ Himself say, *Look unto me, and be ye saved, all the ends of the earth* (Isaiah 45:22)? Looking gives you a claim – and if you can see Him, He is yours.

Love, a burning stream: I was about to compare my Lord's heart with a volcano constantly streaming with the burning lava of love. Oh, that my soul could only get that stream poured into it to set my entire nature on fire, to consume me in the flames and torrent of love!

Love, call of: When the sun visits the flowers that have hidden themselves away in the cold earth to escape from hungry winter, it begins to call them out of their hiding places by shining upon them. Then they eventually say to themselves, "Let us break our bands of sleep asunder. Let us lift up the mold that covers us. Let us peep forth that we may see the blessed sun, for very certainly it is calling us."

Love changes: It is wonderful what a difference love makes in the person who is possessed with it. A poor timid hen that will fly away from every passerby still loves its offspring, and when it has its chicks near it, it will fight like a very griffin for its young. And when the love of Christ comes into a timid believer, how it changes him!

Love conquers: It was not because Moses's rod had smitten the rock, but because Christ's voice of love had spoken to it that the rock dissolved into floods at once! See the summer's sun assail and vanquish the iceberg that has floated from its northern home. Winter's fiercest storms could not dissolve the monstrous mountain of ice, nor could a thousand hurricanes and storms break it in pieces; but the sun shot a strange tremor through its heart as soon as it smiled thereon, and every beam that fell from the fair sphere of day shot through it like a dart, until at last, yielding to the mysterious glow, the iceberg lost its hardness of heart, bowed itself from its frigid loftiness, fell into the warm gulf stream, and was no more to be found. Was it not so with you when the eyes of Jesus darted love into your hearts?

Love, little but real: A little pearl is a pearl as much as a great pearl, though all of us would prefer the greater pearl. The Queen's image is on a sixpenny piece as much as on a sovereign, though all would prefer the golden coin. The image of God is on all His people's faith and love, whether great or small. The main thing with a coin is to be sure it is genuine metal. In the same way, if love is real love, that is the main point.

Love of God: Divine love had no beginning. Those faraway stars are infants whose eyes only yesterday were open to the light, and those mountains are infants newly born; but as for God's love, it is coexistent with His own existence, and the objects of it are always the same.

Love of God: The heart of God never does anything in weakness. His love is strong and powerful, for it is the affection of an omnipotent spirit. Remember the words of the Lord Jesus: *As the Father hath loved me, so have I loved you* (John 15:9). Do you know how much the Father loves His Son? Can you have any idea? Are you not baffled in the attempt? *So,* says Jesus, *have I loved you.*

Love of God: Oh, blessed, blessed be the love of God, to think it would come to us when we were not seeking it, that it came to us unbought and undeserved, spontaneously leaping up like a living fountain with none to dig the well, but springing up in the midst of the Sahara of our barren nature, and then blessing us with unspeakable blessings as it overflowed!

Love shown to the least: No matter how little you may be, it makes no difference in regard to God's love to you. Ask yourselves if you love that full-grown son of twenty-five so much that you have less love for that little angel of two or three years. Bless his little heart – when he climbs upon your knee today and asks whether you have a kiss for him or not, will you answer, "No, Johnny, I cannot love you because you are so little. I give all my love to your older brother because he knows so much more than you do and can be so useful to me"? Oh, no, you love the last one better than any, perhaps, and certainly not less. They say if there is a child in the family who is a little bit weak, the mother always loves him best. It is so with our God; He is most gracious to the weakest and least known.

Love your enemies: When Dr. Duff first read to some young Brahmins in the government school the precept *Love your enemies, bless them that curse you, do good to them that hate you, and pray for them which despitefully use you* (Matthew 5:44), one of the Brahmins cried out, with delight, "Beautiful! Beautiful! This must have come from the true God. I have been told to love those who love me, and I have not always done that; but to love my enemies is a divine thought." That young man became a Christian under the influence of that precept. Let your goodwill go forth even to the worst of people, for Christ's sake. Forget their evil as you behold His goodness.

Luxury conquers: What the arms of Rome could not do against Hannibal, his Capuan holidays are said to have accomplished: his soldiers were conquered by luxury, though invincible by force. When the church lies down at ease, she is likely to feel the diseases of abundance.

* * * *

- Let your wishes blaze up into prayers.

- Like a young bird in its nest, glory dwells in grace.

- Longing follows on the heels of loving.

- Look well to your integrity, and the Lord will look to your prosperity.

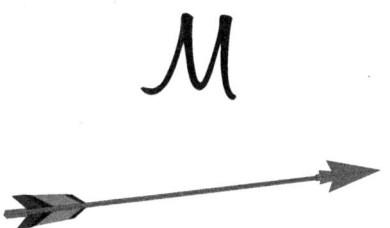

Man, difficult to get at: There is nothing as difficult to get at as a man. You may hunt a badger and run down a fox, but you cannot get at a man, for he has so many tricks and hiding places. Yet the Word of God will dig him out and seize on him. When the Spirit of God works with the gospel, the man may dodge and twist, but the preaching goes to his heart and conscience, and he is made to feel it and to yield to its force.

Man, God's friend: Parmenio was a great general, but all his fame in that direction is forgotten in the fact that he was known as the friend of Alexander. He had a great love for Alexander as a man, whereas others only cared for him as a conqueror and a monarch. Alexander recognized this and placed great reliance upon Parmenio. Abraham loved God for God's sake, and he followed Him fully, and so the Lord made him His confidant. God found pleasure in manifesting Himself to him, and in trusting to him His sacred oracles. O Lord, how excellent is Your lovingkindness that You would make a man Your friend!

Meditation, needful: A person who wants to see a country must not hurry through it by express train, but he must stop in the towns and villages and see what is to be seen. He will know more about the land and its people if he walks the highways, climbs the mountains, stays in the homes, and visits the workshops than if he travels so many miles in a day and hurries through picture galleries as if death were pursuing him. Don't hurry through Scripture, but pause for the Lord to speak to you. Oh, for more meditation!

Memory of friends: Years ago, when sailors used to go to India, they would give as a toast when they left, "To our friends astern," but when they had reached halfway on the voyage, they changed it, and said, "To our friends ahead." When we are midway on our voyage, we are bound to remember our friends ahead.

> E'en now by faith we join our hands
>> With those who went before,
> And greet the blood-besprinkled bands
>> On the eternal shore.[9]

Men, catching: I sometimes hear about people getting very angry after a gospel sermon, and I say to myself, "I am not sorry for it." Sometimes when we are fishing, the fish gets the hook into its mouth. He pulls hard at the line. If he were dead, he would not do so, but he is a live fish, worth the getting. Although he runs away for awhile, with the hook in his jaws he cannot escape. His very wriggling and anger show that he has got the hook, and the hook has got him. Have the landing net ready; we will soon land him. Give him more line; let him spend his strength, and then we will land him – and he will belong to Christ forever.

Mercy, infinite: When a child of God thinks he has exhausted the patience and mercy of God, he is something like a little fish in the sea that said, "Oh, I am so thirsty. I am afraid I will drink up the whole Atlantic Ocean!" O little fish, you have no idea how mighty the ocean is. Countless multitudes such as you may swim in it, and the ocean will not be any less! O beloved believer, you never need to think that you will exhaust infinity!

Message, not to be judged by messenger: Certain of the friars in Martin Luther's day confessed that much of what Luther said was very true and

---

9   This is from a hymn by Charles Wesley (1707-1788) that begins with "Come, let us join our friends above.

reformation was certainly very much needed. However, they did not want to hear it from such a fellow as Luther – a renegade monk who spoke so rudely. Erasmus could be endured, but Luther made such a noise about it. Teaching is often judged not by its own value, but by the prejudices that people may happen to have concerning the source from which it comes. "I do not like him," someone says. Well, what does it matter whether you like him or not? What does he say? If something is true, never mind who says it; believe it.

Minding earthly things: I have heard of a person who walked some seven hundred miles to see Niagara Falls. When he was within seven miles of the Falls, he thought he heard the roar of the waterfall, and he called to a man working in the fields and said, "Is that the roar of Niagara?"

The man said, "I don't know, but I guess it may be. What if it is?"

With surprise, the good man said, "Do you live here?"

"Born and bred here," the man answered.

"And yet you don't know whether that thundering noise is from the waterfall?"

"No, stranger, I have never seen those falls. I look after my farm."

No doubt there are many within the sound of heaven's greatest joys who have never cared to know them. They hope they are saved, but they don't care for great joy. They dig their potatoes. They use their spade and their hoe, but the Niagara is nothing to them. Many people look well to this life, but do not drive themselves to gain present spiritual joy.

Minding earthly things: Many people who have seen themselves in the mirror of the Word have no further thoughts of themselves. Tomorrow morning they will be over head and ears in business. The shutters will be down from their shop windows, but they will be put up over the windows of their souls. Their work needs them, and therefore their prayer closets cannot have them. Their ledgers and bills fall like an avalanche over their Bibles. They have no time to seek the true riches, for fleeting trifles monopolize their minds. You call earthly things "business," but the salvation or damnation of your souls is such a trifling matter to you that any stray hour will suffice for it.

Minds, like stained glass: Some minds are like stained-glass windows. They keep out much of the light, and the little light that does struggle through, they color after their own manner. It is good to be plain glass so that the Lord's light, with all its color and delicacy of shade, may come in just as it comes from heaven, with nothing gathered from ourselves.

Minister's duty: Augustine desired to be always found *aut precantem, aut predicantem*; that is, either praying or preaching, either speaking to God for people in prayer, or speaking for God to people in his ministry. Ministers of Christ, especially, should give themselves not to serving tables, but to the ministry of the Word and prayer (Acts 6:2, 4). For us to give ourselves to promoting entertainment or to compete with theaters and music halls is a great degradation of our holy office. If I heard of a minister becoming a chimney sweep to earn his living, I would honor him in both his callings; but for God's watchmen to become the world's showmen is a pitiful business.

Ministers, guides: Stars are guides, and so are the Lord's true ministers. Some stars in the sky have done measureless service to wanderers over the trackless deep and to those who have lost themselves in the labyrinths of the forest. That pole star has conducted many slaves to liberty. Happy have been the influences of the stars upon the hopeless who, being lost, have laid themselves down to die! Blessed are those men who, shining with the light of God, have turned many to righteousness; will they not shine as the stars forever and ever (Daniel 12:3)? Are there not preachers of the Word who have stood like that famous star over the place *where the young child was* (Matthew 2:9)? They have first led strangers to Jesus, and then have remained in faithful love shining over the place where the Lord abides.

Misunderstood: I heard of a man who lived in a certain town who was greatly misunderstood while he lived. It was known that he had a large income, yet he lived a miserly life, and there were many rumors about the little help he gave to those around him. He scrimped in many ways and hoarded his money. But when he died, the popular verdict was reversed, for then the motive of all his frugality was made known. He left his fortune to build a reservoir and an aqueduct in order to bring a constant supply of pure water to the town where he had been despised and misunderstood. This was the main need of the people, and for a long time they had suffered much from drought and disease because of the meager supply.

All the years that they had misjudged him, he was silently and unselfishly living for their sakes. When they discovered his motive, it was too late to do anything for him other than to hand down to future generations the memory of his noble and generous deed. But we can do much for His sake who has brought to us the living water, and who, although He died for us, is now alive again and will live forevermore.

Models should be perfect: The artist must have a perfect model to copy. Even if the model is not exactly perfect, the artist will do much better than if he had an inferior model to work by. Once a person reaches his own ideal, it is all over with him. A great painter once had finished a picture, and he said to his wife, with tears in his eyes, "It is all over with me. I will never paint again. I am a ruined man."

She asked, "Why?"

"Because," he said, "that painting contents and satisfies me. It realizes my idea of what painting should be, and therefore, I am sure my power is gone."

Jesus Christ is perfect in redemption and holiness, there is no need for another Redeemer.

Moments, use of spare: As goldsmiths sweep up the very dust of their shops so that no filings of the precious metal may be lost, so does the Christian man, when filled with the Spirit, use his brief intervals. It is wonderful what may be done in spare minutes. Little spaces of time may be made to yield a great harvest of usefulness and a rich revenue of glory to God! May we be filled with the Spirit in that respect!

Murmuring, senseless: I know a person who is always grumbling, and I do not wonder that he always seems to have a reason for it. It is like the child who was crying, and his mother said, "Hold your tongue; if you cry for no reason, I will soon give you something to cry about." Many children of God have found something to cry about as the result of senseless murmuring.

* * * *

- Make inscrutable mysteries into footstools for faith to kneel upon.

- Man's security is the devil's opportunity.

- Maturity comes by affliction.

- Men may fast from bread so that they may gorge themselves on pride.

- Men of faith are not idle men.

- Men's pennies and God's promises don't very well go together to buy heaven.

- Merchants generally continue in that business that pays them well, for they feel that they might go further and fare worse. *Return unto thy rest, O my soul; for the* Lord *hath dealt bountifully with thee* (Psalm 116:7).

- Mind your jots and tittles with the Lord's precepts.

- Mindless worship is easy, but worthless.

- Mount like the lark to your God, and sing as you rise.

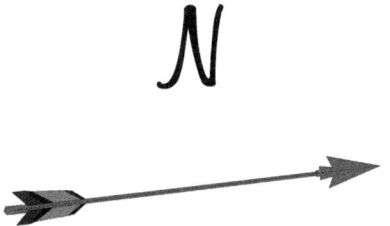

Nearness to Christ: I have heard that in the old times, when they wanted to attract doves to a certain dove house, they took certain birds and smeared their wings with a costly perfume and sent them forth. Other doves were so delighted with their sweetness that they followed them to the dove coops. Oh, that you and I may be so sweetened by dwelling near Christ so that others may come with us to see Jesus and His love!

Need, your strongest plea: I once gave a man a pair of shoes because he said he was in need of them, but after he had put them on and had gone a little way, I saw him in a doorway taking them off in order to go barefooted again. I think they were patent leather, and what would a beggar do in such attire? He was changing them for *old shoes and clouted* (Joshua 9:5). Those were suitable to his business. A sinner is never so well dressed for pleading as when he comes in rags.

Neglected grace: The old story tells of a monarch who gave a ring to a favorite court attendant that he could send to her in case he would be under her displeasure, promising that at the sight of it he would be restored to favor. That ring was never shown, though long waited for, and it was little wonder that, concluding the offender to be stubbornly rebellious, the sentence of execution was carried out. He who never seeks for mercy has certainly never found it.

New creatures: I remember reading a famous writer's description of a miserable cab horse that was old and worn out, yet kept on its regular round of work. They never took him out of harness for fear they would never be able to get his poor old carcass into it again. He had been in the shafts for so many years that they feared if they took him out of them, he would fall to pieces, so they let him remain where he was accustomed to be.

Some people are just like that. They have been in the shafts of sin so many years that they think that if they were once to change, they would fall to pieces. But it is not so, old friend. We are persuaded better things of you – things that accompany salvation. The Lord will make a new creature of you. When He cuts the straps and brings you out from between those shafts that have so long held you, you will forget your old self.

New Year: It is only in imagination that there is any close of one year and beginning of another, yet it has most appropriately all the force of a great fact. When people "cross the line," they find no visible mark. The sea bears no trace of an equatorial belt, yet mariners know where they are, and they take notice of it so that a man can hardly cross the line for the first time without remembering it to the day of his death. We are crossing the line now. We have sailed into another year of grace. Therefore, let us keep a feast unto the Lord. If Jesus has not made us new already, let the new year cause us to think about the great and needful change of conversion.

"Nil desperandum": A man was heard at a prayer meeting pleading in louder tones than usual. He was a sailor, and his voice was pitched to the tune of the roaring billows. A lady whispered to her friend, "Is that Captain F___?"

"Yes," said the other "Why do you ask?"

"Because," she said, "the last time I heard that voice, its swearing made my blood run cold. The man's profanity was beyond measure terrible. Can it be the same man?"

Someone observed, "Go and ask him."

The lady timidly said, "Are you the same Captain F___ whom I heard swearing in the street outside my house?"

"Well," he said, "I am the same person, and yet, thank God, I am not the same!"

O brethren, such were some of us; but we are washed, we are sanctified (1 Corinthians 6:11)! Wonders of grace belong to God. I was reading a story the other day of an old shepherd who had never attended a place of worship, but when he had grown gray and was close to death, he was drawn by curiosity into the Methodist chapel, and all was new to him. Hard-hearted old fellow as he was, he was noticed to shed tears during the sermon. He had obtained a glimpse of hope. He saw that there was mercy even for him. He laid hold on eternal life at once. The surprise was great when he was seen at the chapel, and greater still when, on the Monday night, he was seen at the prayer meeting. Yes, and he was heard at the prayer meeting, for he fell down on his knees and praised God that he had found mercy. Do you wonder that the Methodists shouted, "Bless the Lord"?

Wherever Christ is preached, the most wicked men and women are made to sit at the Savior's feet, clothed and in their right minds (Mark 5:15). My hearer, why should it not be so with you? At any rate, we have full proof of the fact that being a sinner is no reason for despair.

"No God's Land": If an area could be found wherein there would be no God, what a fine building speculation might be made there. No doubt, millions would emigrate to "No God's Land" and would feel at ease as soon as they walked its ungodly shores.

No time for religion: I remember hearing an old lady say to a man who said that he had no time, "Well, you have got all the time there is." I thought that was a very conclusive answer. You have had the time, and you still have all the time there is; why do you not use it? Nobody has more than twenty-four hours in a day, and you have no less.

Now, no time like the present: I subscribe to a religious newspaper from America, and the last copy I received contained these words at the end, in good large type, printed in a practical, businesslike, American way: "If you do not want to have this paper, discontinue it NOW. If you wish to have it for the year 1875, send your subscription NOW. If you have any complaint against it, send your complaint NOW. If you have moved, send a notice of your change of residence NOW." There was a big "NOW" at the end of every sentence. Well, I thought, that's right, and that is common sense. If you want to forsake your sins, forsake them NOW. If you desire mercy from God through Jesus Christ, believe on Him NOW.

* * * *

- Never be afraid of your Bibles.

- Never get an inch beyond the cross.

- No one needs to stick in the mud because he becomes a Christian.

- Nothing holds a man like the silken cord of gratitude.

- Nothing shakes prison walls and breaks jailers' hearts like the praises of the Lord.

O

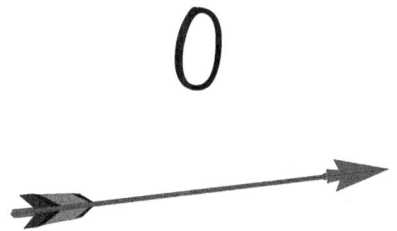

Obedience: You are God's creature, yet you have rendered to Him no obedience! You would not keep a horse or a dog that did not do you some service or follow at your whistle.

Obedience: One man said, you remember, that if God told him to go through a wall, whether he could go through it or not was no business of his. "Here I go," he said, "right at it." We may rest assured that the Lord never commanded us to go through a wall without causing it to give way when our faith brought us to the test. We must obey the command and leave the consequences. If God says, "Do it," the command is both the authorization for our act and the security for our being aided with all necessary help.

Obedience, orderly: It is never good to put Christ's commands out of order, because then they mean just nothing. You have heard of Mary, when her employer said, "Mary, go into the parlor and sweep and dust it." Her mistress went into the parlor and found it dusty. She said, "Mary, did you not sweep the room and dust it?"

"Well, ma'am, yes, I did; only I dusted it first, and then I swept it."

That was the wrong order, and it spoiled the everything.

Old and new theology: I have been informed by those who know most about it that the theology of the future has not yet crystallized itself sufficiently to be defined. As far as I can see, it will take a century or two before its promoters have beaten it into shape, for they have not yet settled which shape it is to be. While the grass is growing, the steed is starving. The new bread is baking and the yeast is well mixed with it, but the oven is not very hot and the dough is not turned into a loaf yet. I should advise you to keep to that bread of which your fathers ate, the bread that came down from heaven. Personally, I am not willing to make any change, even if the new bread were ready on the table, for the new bread is not very digestible, and the yeast of doubt is not according to my desire. I will keep to the old manna until I cross the Jordan and eat the old corn of the land of Canaan.

Old nature remains: A respectable man whom I know said that the other night he was driving along with his old horse. Another man came through the fog, and their horses touched each other, but, he said, "We passed very civilly." Then there came along one like a gentleman, driving rather fast. He drove into the poor man's cart, and instead of making any apology, he cut him across the face with his whip. My friend is a firm Christian, yet he felt the old nature in him and wanted to give the man a cut with his whip in return, but he did not. When he got home, he said, "The old man is not yet dead; if he had been, I would not have felt a momentary spite. I kept him down, but I felt very angry, and I said to myself, 'Although you have been a Christian for a great many years, the old man is still alive.'"

So he is alive in each one of us. He lies like a sneak in the corner, but the day will come when there will be no remains of the evil, no trace of sin left in us, and in heaven we will sing, "He has *washed us from our sins in his own blood*" (Revelation 1:5). He has taken the last trace of sin away, every tendency to evil and every possibility of evil, for it is written, *They are without fault before the throne of God* (Revelation 14:5), and no sin will ever come into their hearts again.

Old things passed away: Dr. Chalmers, in his exposition of Romans, pictures a man engaged with full and diligent ambition on some humble walk of retail merchandise. He cares about little things and makes great account of his small inventory. His hopes and fears range within his limited trading, and he aspires to nothing more than to earn a few dollars a week to retire on. But a splendid property is willed to him, or he is introduced into a surprising walk of high and honorable adventure.

From then on, everything is made new. The man's cares, hopes, habits, tastes, and desires are all new. His expenses change. His valuation of money changes. His fears about the state of his inventory disappear. His joy in the prospect of a small income is no more before his eyes. He has risen to an entirely different level. New conditions have silently changed all things. The whole man is built on a bigger scale. His house, his table, his garments, and his speech are all of another sort. In the same way, the Lord, by all that He has done for us and in us, has changed everything.

Omitted duty: Omitted duty is like a little stone in the sole of your shoe. It is small, and some say it is an insignificant matter, but it is just because it is so small that it can do so much harm. If I had a large stone in my boot, I would be sure to get it out, but a tiny stone may remain and blister me and lame me. Get the little stones out, or they will hinder your traveling to heaven.

Opposition, helpful: Many, many years ago, a number of people were seen headed toward Smithfield early one morning. Somebody asked, "Where are you going?"

"We are going to Smithfield."

"What for?"

"To see our pastor burned."

"Well, why would you want to see him burned? What can be the good of it?"

They answered, "We are going to see him burn to learn the way."

Oh, that was grand. "To learn the way." The common people of the followers of Jesus learned the way to suffer and die as the leaders of the church set the example. Yet the church in England was not destroyed by persecution, but it became mightier than ever because of the opposition of its enemies.

Order, the right thing in the right order: You know that it spoils even good things when you reverse the right order they should be done in, and as we commonly say, "put the cart before the horse." Great harm always comes from departing from God's method in spiritual things. When the Lord tells you to believe and be baptized, if you are baptized first and then believe, you have upset the scriptural order and have practically disobeyed it; you have not kept to God's Word at all. There is nothing like doing the right thing in the right order.

Our commission, our authorization: The postman frequently knocks at the door as late as ten o'clock. I suppose you want to be asleep. Do you cry out, "How dare you make that noise!"? No, he is the postman, an officer of Her Majesty, and he is sent out with the last mail and must deliver the letters. You cannot blame him for doing that for which he is sent. Go and knock at the door of the careless and the sleepy. Give them a startling word. Do not let them perish for lack of a warning or an invitation. Go on without fear. Your assignment is your authorization.

Our inadequacy glorifies Christ: You see that clever boy in a school. Well, it is not much for a master to have made a clever boy of him. However, here is one who shines as a scholar, and his mother says he had the least potential in the family. All his classmates say, "We used to make fun of him the most. He seemed to have no brains. However, our master somehow has taught him and made him know something that, at one time, he appeared incapable of knowing." Somehow it does seem to be as if our very folly and impotence and spiritual death, if the Holy Spirit shows to us the things of Christ, will go toward increasing that at which the Holy Spirit aims – to greatly glorify Christ.

Our righteousness, lifeless: "See here," they say, "we will make it stand." If I had a corpse here (I am glad that I do not), I would stand it up, and it would fall down. Nevertheless, I would then put its legs a little wider apart. Down it goes. Now I will prop it up. Surely I can make this dead thing stand. But no. It has a tendency to fall, and it falls. Have I not seen a sinner trying to set up the corpse of his own righteousness and make it stand? At last he has been forced to say what the fool said in the old classic: "It lacks something inside," and so it does; for until there is life within, it will not stand. Even so, our righteousness has no true vitality, no life within, and it will not stand.

* * * *

- Obedience is for the present tense.

- One of the best positions in which our heart can be found is at Jesus's feet.

- Our littleness does not alter God's promise.

- Our motto is "With God anywhere; without God nowhere."

- Our vessels are never full until they run over. The little over proves our zeal, tests our faith, casts us upon God, and wins His help.

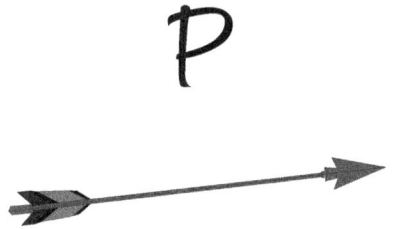

Pardon, free: A prisoner was taken out to die, and as he rode along in the death cart, his heart was heavy at the thought of death, and no one in all the crowd could cheer him. The gallows tree was in sight, and this blotted out the sun for him. But lo, his prince came riding up in hot haste bearing a free pardon. Then the man opened his eyes, and, as though he had risen from the dead, he returned to happy consciousness. The sight of his prince had chased all gloom away. He declared that he had never seen a fairer countenance in all his days, and when he read his pardon, he vowed that no poetry should ever be dearer to his heart than those few lines of sovereign grace. Friends, I remember well when I was in that death cart, and Jesus came to me with a pardon.

Peace: After years of tossing to and fro, Augustine found peace with God by hearing a little child say, "Take up, and read." I suppose that the child was singing to itself and hardly knew what he was saying as he repeated to himself the two words: "*Tolle, lege. Tolle, lege. Tolle, lege.*" "Take up, and read." That voice struck the ear of the perplexed thinker as though it were the voice of God, and he took the Scripture and read the Scripture, and no sooner had he read it than he found Christ. I would ask each one of you to do this so that you might find rest for your soul. Believe what is revealed in Holy Scripture.

Peace, a baseless: A poor woman was the loving mother of an only son. He was very dear to her. He became sick, and was sick unto death; but the mother could not bear to think so. She scraped together the needful fee for a physician, and oh, the peace of heart she had when the trusted man came downstairs and said to her, "Your son will recover; there is no grave cause to fear. Nurse him carefully, and he will soon be at his post again." The mother was restful of heart because she believed the doctor.

Within a single day, her son died, and those hours of false peace were the wormwood and fall of her affliction. It was a sad, sad pity for her hopes to have been raised, for she cried, "If only I had known he was going to die, I would not have felt the loss so severely; but I am grievously disappointed. How could the doctor tell me he would live?" The physician was either greatly mistaken, or else wanted to soothe the mother's obvious anxiety. If the latter was the case, his untruthfulness was unwise. I cannot follow a similar course. It is a pity to create a peace that is baseless.

Peace made with God: I like the language of a poor bricklayer who fell from a scaffold and was so severely injured that he was ready to die. The clergyman of the parish came and said, "My dear man, I am afraid you will die. You had better make your peace with God."

To the joy of the clergyman, the man said, "Make my peace with God, sir! That was made for me upon Calvary's cross centuries ago, and I know it."

Ah, that is it – to have peace that was made by the blood of Christ all those years ago – a peace that can never be broken. Then comes life, and then comes death – yes, a lengthened life and ripe old age comes. The best preparation for a lengthened life is to know the Lord.

Peace, uplifting: The compass on board an iron steamship is placed up high so that it may not be so much influenced by the metal of the ship. Although surrounded by that which would put it out of place, the needle faithfully adheres to the pole because it is set above misleading influence. It is the same with the child of God when the Lord has given him peace. He is lifted beyond the dominion of his sorrowful surroundings, and his heart is delivered from its sad surroundings.

Perfection, modern: You have heard the classic story of the inhabitant of Rhodes who said that at such-and-such a place, he had made a jump of many yards. He bragged until a Greek, who stood by, chalked out the distance, and said, "Would you mind jumping half that length now?" In the same way, I have heard people talk of what enjoyments they once had. I have heard of a man who has the roots of depravity dug out of him; and as for sin, he has almost forgotten what it is. I would like to watch that brother when affected by rheumatism.

I do not want him to have it long, but I would like him to have a twinge or two so that I might see whether some roots of corruption do not remain. I think that when he was tried in that way, or if not just in that way, in some other, he would find that there was a root or two still in the soil. If a storm were to come on, perhaps our brave dry-land sailor might not find his anchor quite so easy to cast overboard as he now thinks it is. You smile at the talk of modern perfection, and so do I; but I am sick of it.

Persecution: When Patrick Hamilton (1504-1528) was burned in Scotland, there was such a catalyst given to the gospel through his burning that the adversaries of the gospel were inclined to say, "Let us burn no more martyrs in public, for the smoke of Hamilton's burning has made many eyes to sting until they were opened." So, no doubt, it always was. Persecution is a red hand that scatters the white wheat far and wide.

Persecution: I was reading the life of John Philpot (1516-1557) the other day. He was locked up in Bishop Bonner's coal hole in Fulham Palace. There he and his friends sang psalms so joyfully that the bishop rebuked them for their joy. They could have quoted apostolic authority for singing in prison. When there were seven of them, Philpot wrote, "I was carried to my lord's coal house again, where I, with my six fellow prisoners, do arise together in the straw as cheerfully, we thank God, as others do in their beds of down."

To be with the people of God, one would not mind being in the coal hole. No one wants to be in Bonner's coal hole, but it is better to be there with the martyrs than upstairs in the palace with the bishop. To hear the saints' holy talk, to sing their joyful psalms with them, and to behold the Angel of the covenant with them is a very different thing from mere suffering or imprisonment.

Perseverance: I am reminded of Sir Christopher Wren (1632-1723) when he cleared away old St. Paul's Cathedral to make room for his splendid building. He was compelled to use battering rams upon the massive walls. The workmen kept on battering and battering. An enormous force was brought to bear upon the walls for days and nights, but it did not appear to have made the least impression upon the ancient masonry. Yet the great architect knew what he was doing. He told them to keep on battering incessantly, and the ram fell again and again upon the rocky wall, until at last the whole mass was disintegrating and coming apart. Then each stroke began to tell. At one blow it reeled, at another it quivered, at another it moved visibly, and at another it fell over amid clouds of dust. Do you think that it was these last strokes that did the work? No, but it was the combination of blows, the first as truly as the last. Keep on with the battering ram.

Personal testimony, helpful: When we meet with someone who has been in special trouble and has escaped from it, we are anxious to know how it came to pass so that if we experience a similar trial, we also may resort to the same door of hope. You meet with someone who has long been severely afflicted, and it is a pleasure and a personal comfort to find him full of joy at his relief. You heard him lamenting for years, and now you hear him rejoicing, and this excites your wonder and your hope.

It is as though a lame man saw another lame man leaping and running. He very naturally inquires, "How did this happen?" The other day you saw a blind man begging in the streets, and now his eyes are as bright as that which sparkles on the face of a gazelle, and you cry in astonishment, "Tell me who was the eye doctor who operated on your eyes, for I may be in a similar situation, and I would be glad to know where to go." Here, then, we have a gate of knowledge opened before us.

Pleasures, sinking sand: There is no real cause for envying the wicked, for their present is danger and their future is doom. I see them now, on that distant island, playing, dancing, and feasting happily. I am standing as on a bare rock, and I might well envy them their island of roses and lilies – but as I watch, I see their captivating island gradually sinking to destruction. The ocean is rising all around. The waves are carrying away the shores. Even while they dance, the floods advance. There is a captivated reprobate sinking amid the devouring flood. The rest of the people continue at their amusement, but it cannot last much longer. They will soon be gone. Let me stand on my lone rock rather than sink amid their fleeting luxury. Let me abide in safety rather than dance where danger is around.

On Christ the solid rock I stand;
All other ground is sinking sand.[10]

Power of truth: A Unitarian minister who preached that wild doctrine of universal salvation once met an old-fashioned Baptist brother who was not a well-educated man, but who had a crowded congregation, while he had only a dozen or two to hear him eloquently speak. The Unitarian said, "I cannot understand how there is such a difference in our congregations; you get so many to hear you, and I so few. I preach a very pleasing doctrine. I tell the people that everything will be right with them at last. I do not worry them with any doctrines of repentance and faith and atonement, yet they will not come to hear me. You preach a very dreary doctrine, and you tell the people that unless they repent they will perish and be cast into hell, yet they crowd your place to hear you. How is that?"

"Well, my friend," said the old man, "I think it is because they have a sharp suspicion that what I say is true, and that what you say is not true."

There he hit the nail on the head. It is so. The conscience of men tells them to distrust the word that tells them there will be no difference between the righteous and the wicked.

Practical Christianity: When a ship first leaves the stocks on which it rests while it is being built, it is good for it to be taken on a trial trip. However, it would be absurd to have a ship always being tried. It is time that it took voyages in real earnest and was registered in the merchant service. There will be then trial enough in the actual execution of service. Some Christians, by continual introspection, are always raising

---

10   This is from the chorus of a hymn by Edward Mote (1797-1874) that begins with "My hope is built on nothing less than Jesus' blood and righteousness."

the point, "Am I a Christian?" Brother, be a Christian. "Am I a child of God?" Brother, be a child of God and enjoy it. Do not spend a lifetime searching for the family register.

Praise, whole-souled: When the photographer fits that iron rest at the back of your head and keeps you waiting about ten minutes while he gets his plates ready, your soul goes out of town, and nothing remains except that heavy look. When the work of art is finished, it is you, and yet it is not you. You were driven out by the touch of that iron. Another time, perhaps, your portrait is taken instantaneously while you are in an animated attitude, while your whole soul is there. Then your friends say, "That is your very self." I want you to bless the Lord with your soul at home just as in that portrait.

I saw a book today in which the writer says in the preface, "We have a portrait of our mother, but there was a kind of sacred twinkle about her eyes that no photograph could reproduce." It is my heart's desire that you praise the Lord with that sacred twinkle, with that feature or ability that is most characteristic of you. Let your eyes praise Him. Let your brow praise Him. Let every part of your manhood be awakened and so stirred up as to be in fine form.

Prayer: We used to have an old member of this church who used to pray in very extraordinary places. Two women were fighting, and he knelt down between them to pray – and they stopped fighting immediately. He has begun to pray in front of a door when there has been a noise in the house. He was better than a policeman, for his prayer shook up the most hard-hearted. They could not understand it. They thought it was a strange thing, and they did not care to put themselves into direct opposition to the man of God. There is a wonderful power in prayer to bless ourselves, besides the blessings that it will bring upon others. Pray with the weak ones, and you will not be a weak one yourself.

Prayer, a begging: You are so troubled that you cannot speak. Well, then, imitate the beggars in the street. They must not beg, for that is contrary to law. But a man sits down and writes on a shovel, "I am starving," and he looks as white as a sheet. What a picture of misery! He is not begging, but the money comes dropping into the old hat. So when you cannot pray, I believe that your silent display of utter inability is the best kind of praying. The blessing comes when we sit down before the Lord, and in sheer desperation expose our spiritual need.

Prayer, ceaseless: The Lord encircles the globe with intercessions by His daily and nightly watchers. As our queen's morning drum beats around the globe, so ceaseless prayer casts a belt of golden grace around the earth.

Prayer, definite: Like a playful boy, you get your bow and arrows and shoot them anywhere. The way to pray is to take in hand the previously mentioned bow and arrows, and – you think I am going to say to shoot them with all your might, but I am not in such a hurry. Wait a bit! Yes, draw the string and put the arrow to it, but wait, wait! Wait until you distinctly see the center of the target! What can be the use of shooting if you do not have something to shoot at? Wait, then, until you know what you are going to do. You want to strike the white, to pierce the center of the target. Be sure, then, that you have got it well into your view!

Imitate David, who says, *In the morning will I direct my prayer unto thee, and will look up* (Psalm 5:3). He has fixed the arrow, drawn the bow, and taken deliberate aim. Now is the time for the next act. He lets the arrow fly. How well directed! See! He has made a bull's-eye! He viewed the mark with his eye, and therefore he has struck it with his arrow. Oh, to pray with a distinct purpose! Indefinite praying is a waste of breath.

Prayer, family: Sir Thomas Abney had been accustomed to have family prayer at a certain time. He was made Lord Mayor of London. As his hour of family prayer was around the same time of a banquet, he asked to be excused for a little while, saying that he had an urgent engagement with a special friend. He then went and called his family together to meet with God in prayer. Do the same. Even if a banquet would be held, leave the table for the altar and your guests for your God.

Prayer never hinders work: In a little church in the Italian mountains, among many absurd paintings, I saw one painting that captivated me. There was a plowman who had turned aside at a certain hour to pray.

The rustic artist drew him on his knees before the opened heavens, and lest there would be any waste of time occasioned by this, an angel was going on plowing for him. I like the idea. I do not think that an angel ever went on with a man's plowing while he was praying, but I think that the same result often comes to pass, and that when we give our hearts to God and seek first the kingdom of God and His righteousness, all these things are added unto us (Matthew 6:33).

Prayer, prevalent: Those who deny the power of prayer never pray. They are not even capable of offering prevailing prayer. Yet these people get up and say it is of no use to pray. They remind me of the Irish prisoner who was brought up for murder, and half a dozen people swore that they had seen him do the deed. "Your lordship," he said, "I could bring you ten times as many people who didn't see me do it." Yes, but that was no evidence at all, and in the same way, these people have the audacity to set up their theory on no better grounds than the fact that they do not pray and God does not hear them.

Prayer, private: A little boy who was accustomed to spend some time every day in prayer went up into a hayloft to pray, and when he climbed into the hayloft, he always pulled the ladder up after him. Someone asked him why he did so. He answered, "Since there is no door, I pull up the ladder" (Matthew 6:6). Oh, that we could always in some way cut the connection between our soul and the intruding things that lurk below!

There is a story told about someone (I never knew who it was) who desired to see me on a Saturday night when I had closed myself up to prepare for the Lord's Day. He was very great and important, and so the maid came to say that someone desired to see me. I told her to say that it was my rule to see no one at that time. Then he was more important and impressive still, and said, "Tell Mr. Spurgeon that a servant of the Lord Jesus Christ desires to see him immediately." The frightened servant brought the message, but the sender gained little by it, for my answer was, "Tell him I am busy with his Master and cannot see servants now."

Prayer, prompted by God: What a gracious God He is! Suppose a great king has been grievously offended by a rebellious subject, but in kindness of heart, he desires to be reconciled. He invites the rebel to ask for pardon. He replies, "O king, I would gladly be forgiven, but how can I properly approach your offended majesty? I am anxious to present such a petition as you can accept, but I do not know how to draw it up."

Suppose this great king were to say, "I will draw up the petition for you." What confidence the supplicant would feel in presenting the petition! He brings to the king his own words. He prays the prayer he is told to pray. By the very fact of drawing up the petition, the monarch pledged himself to grant it.

O, my hearer, the Lord puts it in your mouth to say now, *Take away all iniquity* (Hosea 14:2). May you find it in your heart to pray in that way. That prayer is best that is offered in God's own way and is of God's own urging.

Prayer, to be studied: If I had an invitation to visit the queen and was told I could ask what I pleased of Her Majesty, I would prepare my request. If I wanted to make the most of the interview, I would reflect and set my petition in order. I might ask improperly. I might ask for something inconsistent or something unfit for royalty to bestow. I would therefore carefully consider what to say. When you go before God, it is good to know what you want.

Prayer in fine weather: There was a storm at sea once, and there was a young man on board who was not used to storms, and he fell into a great state of fear. He was not much use on board the ship. He crept into a corner and knelt down to pray, but the captain came along and could not stand that. He shouted, "Get up, you coward; say your prayers in fine weather." He did get up, saying to himself, "I only hope that I may see fine weather to say my prayers in." When he landed, the words the captain said remained in his mind. He said, "That is quite correct. I will say my prayers in fine weather." I would say to you who hope to live a hundred years, say your prayers in fine weather.

Preacher converted by his own preaching: I wish that it might happen to you as it did with my dear friend, Mr. Haslam, whom God has blessed to the conversion of so many. He was preaching a sermon that he did not understand, and while he preached it, he converted himself.

By God's grace, he began to feel the power of the Holy Spirit and the force of divine truth. He so spoke that a Methodist in the congregation called out, "The parson is converted," and so the parson was. He acknowledged it and praised God for it, and all the people sang, "Praise God from whom all blessings flow." His own utterances concerning Christ crucified had been the power of God unto salvation to him.

Preaching remembered by practice: I heard about someone who was asked by her minister whether she remembered last Sunday's sermon. "No," she said, "it is all gone."

"But you should remember it," said the minister.

"No," she replied, "I am not expected to remember it, for you do not remember it yourself; you read it all from a paper."

The argument is that if the preacher does not remember his own preaching to put it into practice, how can he expect others to do so?

Preaching with hands and feet: The religion of mere brain and jaw does not amount to much. We need the religion of hands and feet. I remember a place in Yorkshire, years ago, where a good man said to me, "We have a real good minister."

I said, "I am glad to hear it."

"Yes," he said, "he preaches with his feet."

Well, now, that is a great thing if a preacher preaches with his feet by walking with God and preaches with his hands by working for God.

Precious blood to be used: A gentleman has purchased a very expensive sword with a golden hilt and an elaborate scabbard. He hangs it up in his hall and shows it to his friends. Occasionally he takes it out of the sheath and says, "Feel how sharp the edge is!" The precious blood of Jesus is not meant for us merely to admire and exhibit. We must not be content to talk about it, adore it, and do nothing with it, but we are to use it in the great crusade against unholiness and unrighteousness, until it is said of us, *They overcame him by the blood of the Lamb* (Revelation 12:11).

Prejudice, ears blocked with: I have read that during the reign of Queen Elizabeth, there was a law made that everybody should go to his parish church. But many sincere Romanists loathed to go and hear Protestant doctrine. Through fear of persecution, they attended the parish church, but they filled their ears with wool so that they would not hear what their priests condemned. It is dreary work preaching to a congregation whose ears are blocked with prejudices.

Preparation for the Lord's coming: If I were asked to visit you tomorrow evening, I am sure you would make some preparations for my call, even for someone as commonplace as myself. You would prepare because you would welcome me. If you expected the queen to call, how excited you would be! What preparations a good housewife would make for a royal visitor. When we expect our Lord to come, we will be concerned to have everything ready for Him. I sometimes see the gates open in front of the larger houses in the suburbs, and it means that they are expecting company. Keep the great gates of your soul always open, expecting your Lord to come. It is unproductive to look about for His coming if we never set our house in order and never put ourselves in readiness for His reception.

Presence of God in all things: O child of God, when you are troubled, it is because you imagine that you are alone; but you are not alone, for the Eternal Worker is with you. Listen, and you will hear the revolution of those unmatched wheels that are forever turning according to the will of the Lord. These wheels are high and dreadful, but they move with fixed and steady motion, and they are *full of eyes round about them* (Ezekiel 1:18). Their course is no blind track of a chariot of Juggernaut,[11] but the eyes see, the eyes look toward their end, the eyes look upon all that comes within the circuit of the wheels.

Oh, for a little heavenly eye salve to touch our eyes so that we may perceive the presence of the Lord in all things! Then we will see the mountain to be full of horses of fire, and chariots of fire round about the prophets of the Lord (2 Kings 6:17). The stars in their courses are fighting for the cause of God. Our allies are everywhere. God will summon them at the right moment.

---

11   Juggernaut refers to the Hindu god Jagannath. One Hindu ritual involves wooden images of Juggernaut and other gods being pulled through the streets on large carts or chariots.

Presence of Jesus: Set a bird of the day flying by night, and see how it flutters and how uneasy it is. Go with a candle, if you will, to any place where a number of birds have made their nests, and see how strangely bewildered they are. The only bird that will be at home in the dark is the owl, the bird of the night; and if any of you can be happy without your Master, you are of the night. If you can be content without the sunlight of Jesus's presence, depend upon it that you are one of the bats of the cavern. You are not one of the eagles of the day.

Promise, a key: Sometimes you lose the key to a drawer, and you must have it opened. Therefore, you send for the locksmith, and he comes in with a great bunch of keys. Somewhere among them, he has a key that will open your drawer. The Bible contains keys that will open the iron gates of your trouble and will give you freedom from your sorrow. The point is to find out the right promise, and the Spirit of God often helps us in that matter by bringing the words of the Lord Jesus to our remembrance.

Promises, Christian riches: I heard a story that seemed to me rather an enjoyable one. There was a young woman, fair to look upon, who was seen by a very wealthy gentleman who determined to make her his wife. She had been brought up to habits of rigid thrift, for the family was poor in circumstances. Her father was not one of the poorest, but still, he was poor enough. On her marriage day, he gave her all he could. He added a hundred dollars to her bank account. On the same day, her husband also added ten thousand dollars into the same bank account, and gave her a checkbook so that she could use it for whatever she liked.

Well, having been properly brought up, she spent her own money she had saved very, very carefully. She soon found it gone, however, because of the new circle into which she had been taken. Then she went to the bank to take out fifty dollars in great fear that they would not give it to her. When she had received it, she was surprised and overjoyed. She soon spent this and took out a hundred dollars.

One day her husband said, "You little goose, I thought you did not know how to manage a checkbook."

She said, "Have I been too extravagant?"

"No," he said, "most women would have spent ten thousand dollars, but instead of that, you have only spent one hundred and fifty, and you cannot behave yourself as my wife on such a small amount. Remember, you may be a poor man's daughter, but you are a rich man's wife; so just begin to spend according to my riches, and not your father's thrift."

This is our case in reference to our Lord Jesus. We know we are a poor man's child. Our original father "went broke" long ago. There was nothing left of the family estate. When father Adam was in business, he went bankrupt and left us nothing except a sea of debt. But now we are married to King Jesus, who is heir of all things, and He puts the checkbook of promises into our hands so that we may draw from the riches of divine grace.

Promises are like checks: A promise is like a check. If I have a check, what do I do with it? Suppose I carried it around in my pocket and said, "I do not see the use of this bit of paper. I cannot buy anything with it."

Someone would say, "Have you been to the bank with it?"

"No, I did not think of that."

"But it is payable to you. Have you signed your name on the back of it?"

"No, I have not done that."

"And yet you are blaming the person who gave you the check? The whole blame lies with yourself. Put your name on the back of the check, take it to the bank, and you will get what is promised to you."

A prayer should be the presentation of God's promise endorsed by your personal faith. I hear of people praying about a promise for an hour at a time. I am very pleased that they can, but it is seldom that I feel the need to do so. For me, it is like a person going into a bank with a check and standing there for an hour. The clerks would wonder what you are doing. The commonsense way is to go to the counter, show your check, take your money, and go about your business. There is a style of prayer that is of this fine, practical character. You so believe in God that you present the promise, obtain the blessing, and go about your Master's business.

Promises are like checks: If you had in your house a number of checks that you believed to be good, I do not suppose that you would be unaware of their nature and value for very long. No merchant here would say, "I have a number of checks at home somewhere. I have no doubt that they are all good and that they are my lawful property, but I do not know much about them. Their value is quite unknown to me." Such ignorance would argue insanity. However, will you know your earthly wealth and never consider your heavenly riches? In the Bible there are *exceeding great and precious promises* (2 Peter 1:4). Will it be said that some of God's children do not know what those promises contain? They have read them, perhaps, but they have never really searched into their meaning to see what God has promised.

Promises, personal: When a man sees a garment left at his door that fits him exactly and is evidently cut to suit certain peculiarities of his form, he concludes that the garment was meant for him. Even so, in many promises, I see certain private marks that are the exact counterparts of the secrets of my soul, and these show that God meant me when thus and thus He spoke.

Promises, precious: If you go into the market and are likely to do business, you always take a checkbook with you. In the same way, carry precious promises with you that may plead the word that suits your situation. I have turned to promises for the sick when I have been of that number, or to promises for the poor, the despondent, the weary, and similar things, according to my own condition, and I have always found a Bible verse suited to my own situation. I do not need a promise made to the sick when I am perfectly well. I do not need balm for a broken heart when my soul is rejoicing in the Lord, but it is very convenient to know where to lay your hand upon suitable words of cheer when necessity arises. Therefore, the eternal comfort of the Christian is the Word of God.

Promises, to be tried: Do you think God makes inferior items like some who have made flotation devices that were good to exhibit in a shop but were of no use in the sea? We have heard of swords that were useless in war, and even of shoes that were made to sell but were never made to walk in. God's shoes are of iron and brass, and you can walk to heaven in them without their ever wearing out. You may swim a thousand Atlantics upon His life jacket, and there will be no fear of your sinking. His word of promise is meant to be tried and proved.

Promises, to be used: The other day a poor woman had a little help sent to her, by a friend, in a letter. She was in great distress, and she went to that very friend begging for a few dollars. "Why," said her friend, "I sent you money yesterday, by an order in a letter!"

"Oh dear!" said the poor woman. "That must be the letter that I put behind the mirror!"

In the same way, there are many people who put God's letters behind the mirror and fail to make use of the promise that is meant for them.

Promises, unused: I fear that many of God's promises are seldom used. They are like the locksmith's bunch of keys. Why are they so rusty? Because they are not in constant use. They have not been turned in the lock day by day or they would be bright enough.

Prosperity: Happy is that person who in prosperity can hear the voice of God in the clinking of the sheep bells of his abundant flocks, in the mooing of the oxen that cover his fields, and in the loving voices of dear children around him. However, listen! Prosperity is a painted window that shuts out much of the clear light of God, and only when the blue and the crimson and the golden tinge are removed is the glass restored to its full transparency. Adversity thus takes away tinge and color and dimness, and we see our God far better than before – if our eyes are prepared for the light.

Prosperity: Mr. Jay was never more pleased than when a note was sent to him at Bristol that said, "A young man, who is prospering in business, begs the prayers of God's people so that prosperity may not be a snare to him." Take care that you look in this way upon your prosperity. My dear friend Dr. Taylor, of New York, speaks of some Christians today as having a "butterfly Christianity." When time, strength, thought, and talent are all spent upon mere amusement, what else are men and women but mere butterflies? "Society" is just a group of idle people tolerating each other.

Prove all things: "Oh," someone says, "but you must prove all things." Yes, and I will. However, if someone would set a piece of meat on his table, and it smells rather strong, I would cut a slice, and if I put one bite of it in my mouth and found it too far spoiled, I would not think it is necessary to eat the whole piece of beef to test its sweetness. Some people seem to think that they must read a bad book all the way through, and they must go and hear a bad preacher many times before they can be sure of his quality. No, you can judge many teachings in five minutes. You must say to yourself, "No, sir, no, no, no. This is good meat – for dogs. Let them have it, but it is not good meat for me, and I do not intend to poison myself with it."

Providences: God's ways are at times like heavy wagon tracks. They cut deep into our souls, yet they are all of mercy. Whether our days dash along like the angels mounting on Jacob's ladder to heaven or whether they grind along like the wagons that Joseph sent for Jacob, they are in each case ordered in mercy. I stand by the happy memories of a tried past – as in summer weather when I walk down a green lane. I look at the deep ruts that God's providence made long ago, and I see flowers of mercy growing in them. All the crushing and the crashing were in goodness.

Surely goodness and mercy have followed me all the days of my life (Psalm 23:6). Yes, *all the days of my life* – the dark and the cloudy, the stormy and the wintry, as surely as in *the days of heaven upon the earth* (Deuteronomy 11:21). Brethren, we may sing a song of pure mercy. The paths of God have been to us nothing else but mercy. Mercy, mercy, mercy. *I will sing of the mercies of the LORD forever* (Psalm 89:1).

Providence, special: When John Bunyan was a boy, he was so foolhardy that when an adder rose against him, he took it in his hand and plucked the sting out of its mouth, but he was not harmed. Later in his life, it was his turn to stand sentinel at the siege of Nottingham, and as he was going forth, another man offered to take his place. That man was shot and so John Bunyan escaped death yet again. We would have had no *Pilgrim's Progress* if it had not been for that. Did not God preserve him on purpose so that he would be saved?

There are special interventions of divine providence by which God spares ungodly people, whom He could have cut down long ago as cumberers of the ground (Luke 13:7). Should we not look upon these as having the intention that the barren tree may be cared for yet another year, if perhaps it may bring forth fruit (Luke 13:8-9)?

Puritan and Cavalier: Sin and error have the upper hand so much that we do not know how to assault them. The two great parties in England, the Puritan and the Cavalier, take turns in power, and right now the Cavalier rules most powerfully. At one time, sound doctrine and holy practice had influence, but in these days, loose teaching and loose living are at the front. But our duty clearly lies in sticking to the Word of the Lord and the gospel of our fathers. God forbid that we *should glory, save in the cross of our Lord Jesus Christ* (Galatians 6:14)! By this sign, we will yet conquer.

Putting on the Lord Jesus: I have read of a great man who took two and a half hours to dress himself every morning. In this he showed littleness rather than greatness; but if any of you put on the Lord Jesus Christ, you may take whatever time you need getting ready. It will take you all your lives, brothers and sisters, to fully put on the Lord Jesus Christ (Romans 13:14) and to keep Him on.

* * * *

- Peace and rest are two names for a flower that buds on earth, but is only found in full bloom in heaven.
- Periodical godliness is perpetual hypocrisy.
- Personal experience is more convincing than observation.
- Pleasures that block the road to heaven should be given up.
- Praise makes the happy man the strong man.
- Pray down the sermon, and then pray up the sermon.
- Prayer can never be in excess.
- Prayer is the promise utilized.
- Prayer is the thermometer of grace.
- Preach the cross and plead the blood.
- Providence is God's business.
- Prudence prays with Moses while it fights for Joshua.

Q

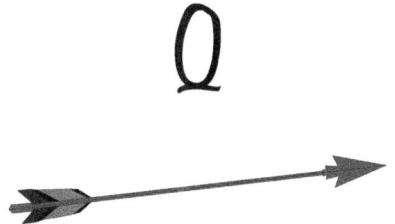

Quakers, honorable title: George Fox (1624-1691), the famous founder of the Society of Friends, was called a "Quaker" for no other reason than that often, when the Spirit of God was upon him and he spoke the Word with power, he would quake from head to foot beneath the burden of the message. It is an honorable title. No man needs to be ashamed to quake when Moses said, *I exceedingly fear and quake* (Hebrews 12:21). In the presence of God, a man may well tremble. He is certainly worse than the devil if he does not, for the devils believe and tremble (James 2:19).

Quietness of mind: A martyr was fastened to the stake, and the sheriff who was to execute him expressed his sorrow that he would persevere in his opinions and force him to set fire to the wood surrounding him. The martyr answered, "Do not trouble yourself, for I am not troubling myself. Come and lay your hand upon my heart and see if it does not beat quietly." His request was complied with, and he was found to be quite calm. "Now," he said, "lay your hand on your own heart, and see if you are not more troubled than I am. Then go your way, and instead of pitying me, pity yourself!" When we have done right, we do not need anyone's pity, no matter how painful the immediate consequences are.

* * * *

- **Question** ruins all melody.

Ready to die: Old George III, who, whatever the faults of his early days, was undoubtedly a godly man in his old age, ordered a mausoleum prepared for himself and his family. When Mr. Wyatt, the architect, went to see him by his own order, he did not know how to speak to the old king about his grave. George said, "Friend Wyatt, do not mind speaking about my tomb. I can talk as freely to you about the preparation of a place for me to be buried in as I could about a room for me to hold my court in. I thank God that I am prepared to do my duty if I live, and to sleep in Jesus if I die." There are only a few, I think, of his rank who could talk in that way, but every wise person should see to it that, since he must die, he is ready for it – ready for the judgment seat of God.

Real life imitated: Multitudes of religious people are like wax figures. They are well proportioned, and you might mistake them by candlelight for living people, but in the light of God you would soon discover a mighty difference, for the best that human skill can do is only a poor imitation of real life. Dressed in the garments of family religion and adorned with the jewels of modern virtue, you may be nothing beyond a child of nature finely dressed, but not the living child. God's living children may not seem to be quite as handsome, not as charmingly arrayed as you are, and in their own esteem they may not be worthy to associate with you, but there is a serious difference between the living child and the dead child, no matter how you may try to conceal it.

Real pleasure: "Well, Jack, old fellow," said someone who met a man who had lately joined the church, "I hear you have given up all your pleasures."

"No, no," said Jack. "The fact lies the other way. I have just found all my pleasures, and I have only given up all my follies." Every Christian can confirm that way of putting it. We who have believed in Jesus have lost no real pleasures, but we have gained immensely in that direction.

Reconciliation: The only way for anyone to understand the joy of reconciliation is to be reconciled himself. Have you heard the story of the boy at the mission house to whom the missionary gave a piece of white sugar? He had never seen it before, and when he reached home, he told his father about this sweet stuff. His father said, "Is it like so-and-so?" The boy could not answer his father's questions, so he ran down the street to the teacher and said, "Teacher, please give me a lump of the white stuff for my father; he wants to know how sweet it is, and I cannot tell him. He must eat it for himself." Reconciliation to God has a sweetness in it that only those who enjoy it can know.

Record kept by God: Our Lord does not call for the time sheet every night, but a time sheet is kept all the same. There will be a day for accountability, and we will have to answer for what we have done.

Reflection of self: The reflection of self in the Word is very much like life. Perhaps you have seen a dog so astonished at his image in the mirror that he has barked fiercely at himself. A parrot will mistake its reflection for a rival. Well may the creature wonder, since every one of its movements is so accurately copied; it thinks it is being mocked. Under a true preacher, people are often so thoroughly unearthed and laid bare that even the details of their lives are reported. Not only is the portrait drawn to life, but it is an actual living portrait that is given in the mirror of the Word. There is little need to point with the finger and say, *Thou art the man* (2 Samuel 12:7), for the hearer realizes on his own that he is spoken of.

Religion, all important: If true religion is important, it is all important. If it is anything, it is everything. If it is false, leave it entirely, and if it is true, love it completely. To show how the joy of religion is proportioned to the degree of it, I sometimes tell a story. It is a parable most instructive and fully to the point, and therefore I cannot help repeating it. It is a story of a man in America who was fond of growing the finest apples. He asked a neighbor to come to his orchard and taste his apples, which he greatly praised as the best in the world. He sang this high praise many times in his friend's ear, but he could not get him to come to his place to taste the fruit. He asked him again and again to come, but he would not. He therefore hinted that there must be a reason for his refusal.

"Well," said the other man, "the truth is that one day I was driving by your orchard and I saw an apple or two that had dropped onto the road. I picked one up and tasted it, and it was, without exception, the sourest thing in creation. I am very grateful to you, but I have had enough for one lifetime."

"Oh!" said the owner, "I traveled forty miles to buy those sour apples, and I planted them all along the border, for I thought they would be good for boys and keep them from stealing the apples. They are a fine type for that particular purpose. But if you will come and see me, I will lead you inside the orchard, past those first two or three rows, and you will find a sweetness and flavor that will fill your mouth with delight."

"I see," said the other, "I see."

Do you also see my meaning? All around the outside of religion, there are sour fruits of prohibitions, rebukes, repentances, and self-denials intended to keep hypocrites out. Have you never seen how long they pull their faces, as if their religion did not agree with them? That is because they have eaten the sour apples on the outskirts. But if you would come near to the faith and joy that are in Jesus Christ, if you would give all your heart to heavenly pursuits, you would find it quite another thing. Then your heart would rejoice with joy unspeakable and full of glory.

Religious ostriches: What numbers of professing Christians I have known who go into one place of worship and hear one form of doctrine and apparently approve it simply because the teacher is "a clever man!" They hear an opposite teaching, and they are equally at home because again, he is "a clever man!" They join a church, and you ask them, "Do you agree with the views of that community?" They neither know nor care what those views may be. One doctrine is as good as another to them. Their spiritual appetite can enjoy soap as well as butter. They can digest bricks as well as bread.

These religious ostriches have a marvelous power of swallowing everything. They have no spiritual discernment, no appreciation of truth. They follow any clever person, and in this they prove that they are not the sheep of our Lord's pasture, of whom it is written, *A stranger will they not follow, . . . for they know not the voice of strangers* (John 10:5).

Religious routine: I have heard of soldiers sleeping while on the march, and I have known some good people to sleep while praying until I have thought that their prayers were a kind of pious snore. They go on with the old phrases without considering what they mean by them. They are like crickets whose notes are always the same. *I sleep,* says the spouse, *but my heart waketh* (Song of Solomon 5:2). However, these people might more truly say, "I do not sleep, and yet my heart is not awake."

Many prayers are like a grocer's account: ditto, ditto, ditto. The petitions are as per usual. It is dreary when we have the shell of a prayer before us but have no oyster in it. The brother's lips are here in prayer, but his soul has gone home to his shop or to his farm. The sails of his mill go around as the wind blows, but he is not grinding anything. There is no grist in the mill; there is no intelligent, loving desire. Let us get out of the ruts of phrases and set petitions. Mere routine religion is abhorrent, yet how easily we fall into it. Let us not rest on our oars and hope to make progress by the momentum already gained.

Remembrancer, Lord's: A high office is that of the remembrancer to the King of kings.[12] Every Christian holds this important position. Oriental kings maintained an officer whose business it was to remind the king of those promises he had previously made. He said this to that court attendant, and that to the other, but the king had plenty of things to think about, and therefore, every now and then, his remembrancer would say, "Please, your Majesty, you promised to do this and that; may it please you to perform your word."

The Lord has appointed His praying people to be His remembrancers. I would never have dared to use such an expression if I had not found it in the inspired Word itself. The Lord says in Isaiah 43:26, *Put*

---

12   A remembrancer to the king was a person responsible to bring matters to the attention of the king.

me in remembrance. The Lord cannot forget, but in condescension to our forgetfulness, He tells us to act as if He could do so and to put Him in remembrance. By calling the promise to the Lord's remembrance, we ourselves are made to be better acquainted with it. I find that a remembrancer was also appointed in our English courts to remind the officers of their duty to their sovereign. This is also a part of our work – to remind the world that there is a God, and that He claims obedience from His creatures. Brethren, fulfill your duty.

Repentance: The best anticipation is that which waits with patience. Our esteemed brother Mr. Lockhart tells a story of one of his members by the name of Carey. She was very sick and close to death, but she expressed a desire to live. He was somewhat astonished by this, for he knew her to be so well prepared to depart. She wanted to stay here for a while for a good and commendable reason. There was one thing that she could see here on earth that she could not see in heaven, and she wanted to remain here to see it again and again.

"What is that?" Mr. Lockhart asked.

"It is the tear of repentance on the sinner's cheek. I want to see a great many more of those before I go home."

Repentance, true: I remember the story of Thomas Olivers (1725-1799), the famous cobbler convert who was a loose living man until he was renewed by grace through the preaching of Mr. Wesley. Olivers became a mighty preacher and the author of that glorious hymn, "The God of Abraham Praise." Before he was converted, this man was much in the habit of contracting debts. He says, "I felt as great sorrow and confusion as if I had stolen every sum I owed." He was not repentant for this one debt, or that other debt, but for being in debt at all, and therefore, having a little coming to him from the estate of a relative, he bought a horse and rode from town to town paying everybody to whom he was indebted. Before he had finished his pilgrimage, he had paid seventy debts, principal and interest, and had been forced to sell his horse, saddle, and bridle to do it.

During this eventful journey, he rode many miles to pay a single dollar. It was only a dollar, but the principle was the same whether the debt was a dollar or ten thousand dollars. Just as he who hates debts will try to clear himself of every dollar owed, so he who repents of sin repents of it in every shape. No sin is spared by the true penitent. He abhors all sin.

Reserve of Christians: It is a pity that Christian people so often shut themselves up within themselves. This is a particular fault of English people. You can travel all over the world in the same railway carriage with an Englishman, and he will not say a word to you. Christian people would get much good from one another if they would not be so distant. Many precious children of God have sat side by side for hours at a time, and out of unnecessary restraint, which they have thought most proper, they have failed to communicate and have missed the opportunity of a sacred exchange of thought and experience that would have enriched them both.

Rest at home: Home is the place of special rest. At home we are unloaded of all the world's huge burden. The advocate takes off his gown and says, "Lie there, Mr. Lawyer, and let the father come to the front!" The tradesman takes off his apron, the warrior his uniform, and the laborer his yoke, for he is at home. If a man may rest anywhere on earth, it must surely be in his own home. Is not our God our rest? O beloved, is there indeed beneath the sun any rest for a poor soul except in God? *There remaineth therefore a rest to the people of God* (Hebrews 4:9), and that rest is God Himself. *Return unto thy rest, O my soul; for the* LORD *hath dealt bountifully with thee* (Psalm 116:7).

Rest, greatly needed: In Oliver Cromwell's time, a writer tells us that he walked all down Cheapside in the early morning and found all the blinds down – because at every house they were having family prayer. Where will one go to find such a state of things in this desperate age? You are up in the morning and at it, and all day long you are at it, and at it, and at it. Little rest is given to our minds, yet we need holy rest.

Rest of knowing: I remember well a minister saying to me, "I wish I could feel as you do. You have certain fixed principles about which you are sure, and you only have to state them and enforce them; but I am in a formative state. I make my theology fresh every week." Dear me, I thought, what a hopeless state for progress and establishment! If the student of mathematics had no fixed law as to the value of numbers, but made a new multiplication table every week, he would not make many calculations.

If a baker were to say to me, "Sir, I am always altering the ingredients in my bread. I make up a different recipe every week," I would be afraid that the fellow would poison me one of these days. I would rather go to a man whose bread I had found good and nourishing. I cannot afford to experiment in the Bread of Life. Besides, there is an intellectual unrest in all this kind of thing that is escaped from when we come to love the Word of the Lord as we love our lives. Oh, the rest of knowing within your very soul that the truth you rest upon is a sure foundation!

Restless minds: A mind on wheels knows no rest. It is like a rolling thing before the storm. Struggle against the desire for new doctrine, or it will lead you astray as the will-o'-the-wisp deceives the traveler. If you desire to be useful, if you long to honor God, if you want to be happy, then be established in the truth and do not be carried about by every wind of doctrine in these evil days. *Be ye steadfast, unmovable* (1 Corinthians 15:58).

Restrained from sin: We have not been as bad as some others because we could not be. A certain boy has run away from home. Another boy remained at home. Is he, therefore, a better child? Listen! He had broken his leg and could not get out of bed. That takes away all the credit of his staying home. Some people cannot sin in a certain direction, and then they say to themselves, "What excellent people we are to abstain from this wickedness!" Sirs, you would have done it if you could, and therefore your self-praise is mere flattery. If you had been placed in the same position as others, you would have acted as others have done, for your heart goes after the same idols.

Reward for service: You remember the old Roman Catholic legend that contains a great truth. There was a brother who preached very mightily and who had won many souls to Christ, and it was revealed to him one night in a dream that in heaven he would have no reward for all he had done. He asked to whom the reward would go, and the angel told him it would go to an old man who used to sit on the pulpit stairs and pray for him. Well, it may be so, but both would most likely share their Master's praise. We will not be rewarded, however, simply according to our apparent success.

Riches abused: I knew a brother who, when he had a little money, rejoiced to have it because he gave to the cause of God abundantly. I believe that he is now worth a hundred times as much as he was then, and he gives a hundredth part of what he used to do when he was poorer. In proportion as his pocket has grown golden, his heart has grown hard. He has gone down in himself in proportion as he has gone up in his property, and now he does not enjoy things as he used to do. He is a poor creature compared to what he once was. Even in his own opinion, he is not the happy man he once was.

Ridicule endured: I wonder when I hear some people say, "I cannot stand being laughed at."
   "Does laughter break bones?"
   "But ridicule is very sharp."
   "Is it? Do the wounds bleed?"
   "Well," someone says, "a sharp insult from someone stings!"
   "Does it? Do you have no cure for such bites?"
   In our minds, some of us have been like Marcus Arethusa, who was stung to death by wasps; yet we are none the worse, but rather we are all the better, for there remains no place on which a new sting can operate.

Righteousness: I saw a peddler one day as I was taking a walk. He was selling walking sticks. He followed me and offered me one of the sticks. I showed him mine – a far better one than he had to sell – and he withdrew at once. He could see that I was not likely to be a purchaser. I have often thought of that when I have been preaching. I show people the righteousness of the Lord Jesus, but they show me their own righteousness, and all hope of dealing with them is gone. Unless I can prove that their righteousness is worthless, they will not seek the righteousness that is of God by faith (Romans 3:22).

* * * *

- Real faith will find a way out of perplexity or will make one.

- Religion without a heart is a terrible thing.

- Remove grace out of the gospel, and the gospel is gone.

- Repentance, apart from Christ, needs to be repented of.

- Repentance puts us in a lowly seat.

- Revivals are our jubilees.

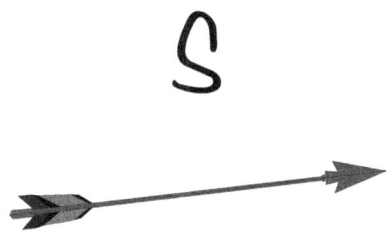

Safety in trusting fully: There is a picture in a quaint old book that represents a man with a whip trying to strike another man, but the man who is attacked runs close in so that the adversary cannot strike him. Run in near to God, and He cannot strike you.

Salvation: The salvation of a single soul is a host of miracles. I heard of a fire that consumed the shop of a jeweler, and a number of costly treasures of gold and silver and precious stones were found among the ruins, caked into a conglomerate of riches. What a treasure! Such is the salvation of a single person. It is a collection of priceless mercies melted into one inestimable piece, dedicated to the praise of the glory of His grace who makes us to be *accepted in the beloved* (Ephesians 1:6) and *saved in the* LORD *with an everlasting salvation* (Isaiah 45:17).

Salvation for today: I was once in a country town, and I said to my host when I went to bed, "I have to be in London tomorrow, and I cannot get up in time for my work unless I leave by a train that I can catch easily enough if you wake me at six."

Well, my host was an Irishman, so he woke me at five o'clock and told me I only had another hour to sleep. The consequence was that I missed my train. If he had only woke me up at the proper time and said, "Now you must get up," I would have dressed at once; but since he said, "You have only another hour to sleep," of course I slept, being weary.

The same principle applies to you. If I say to you, "Go home and think it over all week," I will be giving you a week in which to rebel against God, and I have no right to do that. I will be giving you a week to continue as an unbeliever, and he who is an unbeliever is in danger of eternal ruin, for *he that believeth not shall be damned* (Mark 16:16). Worse than all, the week may lead to many other weeks, to months, maybe years, and then possibly a whole eternity of torment.

I cannot let you have even five minutes. God the Holy Spirit speaks by me now to souls whom God hath chosen from *before the foundation of the world* (Ephesians 1:4), and He says, *Today if ye will hear his voice, harden not your hearts* (Hebrews 4:7). The Holy Spirit says, "Today – even today."

Salvation, full: When I trusted Christ, I did not trust Him to save me for a year or two, but forever. When you go on the heavenly journey, take a ticket all the way through. Some of our friends take a ticket to the next station, and then rush out to get another. Take your ticket for the new Jerusalem and not for somewhere in between. The train will never break down, and the track will never be torn up. If you trust Jesus Christ to carry you through to glory, He will do it.

"Saved alone": Not long ago, we heard of the shipwreck from which a mother was washed on shore, but found all her children drowned. She telegraphed to her husband two words. The first was pleasant to his eye: "Saved." The next was full of misery: "Alone."[13] Would you or I like to have it so – "Saved alone"? God forbid! When we reach heaven's gate, may we be able to say, "Here am I and the children that You have given me" (see Isaiah 8:18; Hebrews 2:13).

Saved, a sinner: A certain youth was at a common playhouse. A scene occurred in which a mutinous sailor was to be hanged, and asking for a glass of spirits, he was represented as drinking his own health in the words, "Here's to my immortal soul." "Immortal soul," thought the foolish youth – "immortal soul!" He had almost forgotten that he had an immortal soul. It was a shot fired at the center of the target. It struck him

---

13　This telegraph was from Anna Spafford to her husband, Horatio, the author of the hymn "It Is Well with My Soul."

home. He was ready to drop. He sought the open air and a place where he could weep. The next Lord's Day morning found the young reprobate at a prayer meeting seeking his father's God. Before long, he found peace through the blood of Jesus and began preaching the gospel that he had so grievously abused. God knows how to get at the heart of sinners.

Savior for sinners: If you put two canaries in a cage tonight, and in the morning when they awake they see some seed in a box, what will the birds do? Will they stop and ask what the seeds are there for? No, but each reasons like this: "Here is a little hungry bird, and there is some seed; these two things go well together." And immediately they eat. In the same way, say, "Here is a Savior, and here is a sinner; these two things go well together. Dear Savior, save me, a sinner!"

Scripture landmarks: When a text stands in the middle of the road, I drive no farther. The Romans had a god they called Terminus, who was the god of landmarks. Holy Scripture is my sacred landmark, and I hear a voice that threatens me with a curse if I remove it. Sometimes I say to myself, "I did not think to find this truth to be just so, but since it is, so I must bow. It is rather awkward for my theory, but I must alter my theology, for the Scripture cannot be broken." *Let God be true, but every man a liar* (Romans 3:4). We want our children to have this deep reverence for Scripture, even as we have it ourselves.

Scripture warnings: A precept of Scripture is like a lighthouse upon a rock; it quietly tells the wise helmsman to steer his vessel another way. The whole coast of life is guarded by these protecting lights, and he who will take note of them will have safe navigation. Remember that it is one thing for the Scripture to give warning, and another for us to take it. If we do not take warning, we cannot say, *By them is thy servant warned* (Psalm 19:11).

Sealed testimony: In olden times, people did not often write their names because they could not write at all. Even kings set their seals because they could not give a signature. To this day, it often happens to me as a trustee of a chapel or school to have a paper laid before me, and I not only sign my name, but I put my finger on that red wafer, which represents my seal, and I say, "This is my act and deed!" When you believe in Jesus, you have set your seal to the testimony of Jesus, which is the revelation of the Lord. You have certified that you believe in God as true.

Season, a convenient: When the countryman wanted to cross the river and found that it was deep, he sat down by the bank to wait until the water had gone past. He waited, but the river was just as deep after all his waiting. With all your delay, the difficulties in the way of your accepting Christ do not become any less. If you look at the matter properly, you will see that there are no great difficulties in the way, nor were there ever such obstacles as you imagined. Another countryman who had to cross Cheapside Street one morning was so confused by the traffic of omnibuses and cabs and people that he felt sure he could not get across then, so he waited until the people and traffic thinned, but all day long it was the same. Unless he had waited until the evening, he would have found little difference. Oh, friends, you have waited for a convenient season to become a Christian, and after all your delay, the way is no clearer.

Secular united to the sacred: In the days of Queen Mary, a foolish person dug up the bones of the wife of Martin Bucer out of spite. Poor woman! She had done nothing wrong, except that she had married a teacher of the gospel, but she was dragged from her grave to be buried in a dunghill for that offense. When Elizabeth came to the throne, Mrs. Bucer's bones were buried again, but to make the body secure from any future malice of bigots, our prudent forefathers took the relics of a certain popish saint, who was enshrined at Oxford, and mixed the remains of the two deceased persons past all chance of separation. In this way, Mrs. Bucer was secured from further disrespect by her unity with the body of one of the canonized.

I want the secular to be secured like this by union with the sacred. If we could only feel that our common acts are parts of a saintly life, they would not so often be done carelessly. If we lay our poor daily life by itself, it will be disregarded; but if we combine it with our holiest ambition and exercises, it will be preserved. Our religion must be part and parcel of our daily life, and then the entirety of our life will be preserved from the destroyer. Does not the Scripture say, *Whether therefore ye eat, or drink, or whatsoever ye do, do all to the glory of God* (1 Corinthians 10:31)?

Self-complacency: Self-complacency is the mother of spiritual decay. David said, "My mountain stands firm. *I shall never be moved*" (Psalm 30:6-7), but before long, the face of God was hidden, and he was troubled. In the presence of a professing Christian who is pleased with his own attainments, one remembers that warning text: *Let him that thinketh he standeth take heed lest he fall* (1 Corinthians 10:12).

Self-confidence: Listen to a parable. Over there is a river, deep and broad. You imagine that the proper way to cross it is to wade or swim through it. You will not consider any other way. The king has built a bridge. It is open without toll. The passage is as safe as it is plain. You refuse to be beholden to His Majesty. You intend to get across by your own efforts. You are already wet and cold, but you intend to persevere. You are nearly up to your neck in the stream, and the current is too strong for you. Come back, O foolish man. Come back and cross the river by the bridge! The way of faith is so safe, so simple, so blessed. Try it! Have you not had enough of trying to save yourself? After years of struggling, you are no farther forward and have no more comfort. Stop struggling, and rest on the Lord Jesus. Give up your self-confident foolishness and confide in the Son of God, the bleeding substitute for guilty men.

Self-esteem: Self-esteem is a moth that eats the garments of virtue. Those flies, those pretty flies of self-praise, must be killed, for if they get into your pot of ointment, they will ruin it all. Forget the past. Thank God, who has made you pray so well. Thank God, who has made you kind, gentle, or humble. Thank God, who has made you give generously. But forget it all and go forward since there is still very much land to be possessed.

Self-examination: The sailor has been happily on a smooth sea, and he has paid no attention to his bearings. Suddenly he sees a rock ahead. He should have been far away from this. He shortens his sail, looks around him, and changes his course. He sets a better watch and is restless until he reaches the old familiar channel again. Fellow voyager on the sea of life, may not this be your case?

Self-examination: Tradesmen generally give up attention to their account books when things are not in order with them. They do not like their books, for their books do not like them. The person who does not like self-examination may be pretty certain that things need examining.

Self-made Christians: I read a book one day called *Self-Made Men*, and in its own sphere it was excellent, but spiritually I would not like to see a self-made man. He would be an awful specimen of humanity. A self-made Christian is one of the kind that very soon the devil takes, as I have seen children take a bran doll and shake it all out. Satan likes to shake out self-made Christians until there is nothing left of them.

Self-righteous: Our own supposed fullness keeps us from receiving Christ's fullness. It must be so. You may remember the story of the plowman and Mr. James Hervey. The plowman asked Mr. Hervey what he thought the greatest hindrance was to people's salvation. Mr. Hervey replied, "Sinful self."

"No," said the plowman, "I think righteous self is a greater hindrance to people's salvation than sinful self. Those who are sinful will come to Christ for forgiveness, but those who think they are righteous never will."

The full oil jar can hold no more. A deserving sinner (if such a person could exist) would be of no use to the Savior, and the Savior could be of no use to him.

Self-righteousness: The man upon whom there is found a counterfeit coin is very sincere in declaring that it is not his. He insists that somebody must have slipped it into his pocket. He will not admit that it is his. A little while ago he thought to himself, "What a splendid imitation it is! How well I have cheated the queen!" Self-righteousness is nothing but a counterfeit coin, and when all goes well with us, we say, "How well I have done it! How splendid is my righteousness!" However, when the Spirit of God gets our attention, then we are anxious to get rid of the very thing in which we gloried. What we used to consider to be our righteousness we now consider to be as filthy rags (Isaiah 64:6) – and we consider according to truth.

Self-salvation, impossible: It is with the sinner as with the Roman Catholic Saint Dennis. You have heard the old fable that when he had his head cut off, he picked it up and walked a thousand miles with it in his hand. A scoffer said that the thousand miles' walk was nothing much, for it was only the first step that had any hardships in it. In the same way, when a soul goes to heaven, if it takes the first steps in its own strength, it can walk all the way; and then it will have all the glory.

Self-satisfaction: Whatever shape self-satisfaction may take (and it takes a great many different shapes), it is at bottom nothing but avoiding the hardship of the life of a Christian soldier. The Christian soldier has to fight with sins every day, and if he is a man of God and if God's Spirit is in him, he will find that he needs all the strength he has, and a great deal more, to maintain his ground and make progress in the divine life.

Self-surrender, reciprocal: You remember how Count Zinzendorf was converted to Christ by seeing, at Dusseldorf, Domenico Feti's painting of Christ on the cross, and at the bottom these words:

> All this I did for thee,
> What hast thou done for Me?

I share the question with you, although I cannot paint the picture or make you see the vision. If Christ has redeemed you, then it follows as a matter of course that you will realize that you are not your own, but were *bought with a price* (1 Corinthians 6:20), and you will willingly offer yourself to God.

Sense of need is the best plea: We have an orphanage, and the qualification for our orphanage is that the child for whom admission is sought is entirely destitute. Will a widow, trying to show to me and my fellow trustees that her boy is a suitable object for the charity, tell us that her child has a rich uncle? Will she enlarge upon her own abilities to earn a living? This would be to argue against herself. So, sinner, do not pretend to be righteous. Jesus comes to make the ungodly godly and the sinful holy.

Sermons, still being preached: A sermon should be like a musical box. We wind it up when we preach it, and then it continues playing until its tune is through. It should be said of a good sermon, "It being ended, still speaks." Hear what you hear in such a way that it will be a seed that will grow in the garden of your heart.

Shame, bravely borne: I heard of a prayer the other day that I did not quite like at first, but there is something in it after all. The good man said, "Lord, if our hearts are hard, make them soft; but if our hearts are too soft, make them hard." I know what he meant, and I think I can pray that last prayer for some of my friends who are so delicate that a sneer would kill them. May the Lord harden them until they can despise the shame! Answer shame by making it see that you are ashamed of the scorner. Laugh at the laughter of fools. Despise their despising. With glorious greatness of spirit, Jesus remained unprovoked amid the cruel taunts of godless men. Run through the crude crowd. Shut your ears and run, despising the shame.

Sham sinners: There are many sham sinners about. One day in Italy I saw a fellow sticking out his arm with a terrible sore, and he begged from me. As I suspected that he had manufactured that sore with a little sulfuric acid or by some such process, I did not feel any pity for him. We have lots of people who come confessing their sins. "Oh, yes, we are sinners! We are sinners!" They do not mean it; they are only sham sinners. A real sinner, one who feels his guilt, is a sacred thing. As Joseph Hart said, "The Holy Spirit has made him so."

Signals must be correct: Everything in railway service depends upon the accuracy of the signals. When these are wrong, life will be sacrificed. On the road to heaven, we need unerring signals or the catastrophes will be far more terrible. It is difficult enough to set myself right and carefully drive the train of conduct, but if, in addition to this, I am to set the Bible right, and thus manage the signals along the permanent way, I am in a dreadful situation indeed. If the red light or the green light may deceive me, I am just as well without signals as to trust such faulty guides. We must have something fixed and certain, or where is the foundation?

Silence: If an enemy has said anything against your character, it will not always be worthwhile to answer him. Silence has both dignity and argument in it. Nine times out of ten, if a boy makes a blot in his copy book and borrows a knife to take it out, he makes the mess ten times worse. Since in your case there is no blot after all, you do not need to make one by attempting to remove what is not there. All the dirt that falls upon a good man will brush off when it is dry; but let him wait until it is dry and not dirty his hands with wet mud.

Silence, wisdom of: I think I remember reading about George Fox sitting down with a crowd of people around him for a long time and never saying a word. They were all watching and waiting. If it had been myself, I would have stood up quickly and would have probably said something foolish. But George Fox was a wise man, and he sat still. It takes a very wise man to hold his tongue so long. George Fox kept silence so that he might starve the people from words.

Sin a troubler: Sin is not only fault, but it is foolish. It will be to your own harm as well as to my displeasure. Dear child of God, are you out in the storm just now? Do you have no rest? Let me talk to you. Is there not a cause? Somebody upon your vessel has brought this storm upon you. Where is he? He is not among the regular sailors who work the ship. He is neither captain nor shipmate. He is a stranger. Down under the hatches is a man named Jonah. Is he the cause of the storm? "No," you say, "for he is a good man and has paid his fare." This makes one feel even more suspicious. He is the cause of the mischief. You will never get peace until the Jonah of sin is overboard. Cast him into the sea, and you will find calm.

Sin coming home: I heard the other day of someone in India who was thought to be dead. The Parsee method is not to bury their dead, but they leave them naked in the "Towers of Silence," where there are vultures always waiting. Within three or four hours, there is no flesh on the bones. One poor man who had only passed out, but was thought dead, was laid there. The vultures came, and one or two of them tore his flesh so terribly that he jumped up as from a dreadful dream. There were the vultures coming to devour him while he was still alive, and defending himself as best as he could, he managed to escape. What a predicament to be in – lying in the place of the dead, surrounded by the cruel beaks of those ravenous birds! But in a far more terrible position is a sinner when his sins come home to him. Only the Lord can drive those vultures away and restore him to life and safety.

Sinful delay: To refuse to do right is a great evil, but to continue in that refusal until conscience grows numb in regard to the matter is still worse. I remember a person coming to be baptized who said he had been a believer in the Lord Jesus for forty years and that he had always seen the ordinance to be baptized as scriptural. I felt grieved that he had been so long disobedient to a known duty, and I suggested to him that he should be baptized at once. It was in a village, and he said that there were no conveniences. I offered to go with him to the brook and baptize him, but he quoted Isaiah 28:16 and said, "No, for *he that believeth shall not make haste.*" Here was someone who had willfully disobeyed his Lord for as many years as the Israelites were in the wilderness, upon a matter so easy to perform, yet after confessing his fault, he was not willing to mend it, but misused a passage of Scripture to excuse him in further delay.

Singing in fine weather: Sing in fine weather! Any bird can do that. Praising God when all goes well is ordinary work. Everybody identifies the nightingale above all other birds because she sings when the other minstrels of the wood are silent and asleep, and in the same way, faith praises God under the cloud. Songs in the day are from man, but God Himself gives songs in the night (Job 35:10). Let us sing unto the Lord under the cloud. Let us pour forth His praises in the fires! Let us praise Him under depression. Let us magnify Him when our heart is heavy.

Sin, its complete removal: When Dr. Neale, the eminent Ritualist, took John Bunyan's *Pilgrim's Progress* and Romanized it, he represented the pilgrim as coming to a certain bath into which he was plunged and washed, and then his burden was washed away. According to this doctored edition of the allegory, Christian was washed in the laver of baptism, and all his sins were thus removed. That is the High Church mode of getting rid of sin. John Bunyan's way, and the true way, is to lose it at the cross. Now, notice what happened. According to Dr. Neale's *Pilgrim's Progress*, that burden grew again on the pilgrim's back, and I do not wonder that it did, for a burden that baptism can remove is sure to come again. But the burden that is lost at the cross never again appears, forever.

Sin shows up God's love: The black background of sin makes the bright line of love shine out more clearly. When the lightning writes the name of the Lord with flaming finger across the black brow of the storm, we are forced to see it. In the same way, when love inscribes the cross upon the dark tablet of our sin, even blind eyes must see that *herein is love* (1 John 4:10).

Sins forgiven: A story is told about a soldier who was much distressed by his heavy debts. He was in despair, for he owed a great deal of money and did not know where to get it. He took a piece of paper and made a list of his debts, and wrote underneath, "Who will pay these debts?" The emperor of Russia passed by as the soldier was asleep. He picked up the paper and read it, and being in a gracious mood, he signed it at the bottom, "Nicholas." Was that not a magnificent answer to the question? When the soldier woke up and read it, he could hardly believe his own eyes. "Who will pay these debts?" was the despairing question. "Nicholas" was the all-sufficient answer. We ask, "Who will bear our sins?" The magnificent reply is "Jesus"!

Sin's slavery: If you had a bird here, such as a canary, and it was all free except one leg, it would not be a free bird then. "It is only held by a single bit of cotton," you say. Still the bird is not at liberty. It cannot fly as it pleases. As long as a person is held captive by a single sin, no matter how small it is, he is still in bondage to iniquity. If any single sin binds him or masters him, he is not the Lord's freeman. He is still a slave in the worst form of slavery, for he is under the dominion of evil.

Smooth places, slippery: It would not be wise to pray that we may be completely delivered from trial, although we would like to be. It would be a pleasant thing to have a grassy path all the way to heaven, and never to find a stone in the road – but although pleasant, it might not be safe. If the way were a fine grass, cut every morning with a lawn mower and made as soft as velvet, I am afraid we would never get to heaven at all, for we would linger too long on the road. Some animals' feet are not adapted for smooth places, and brethren, you and I are of a very slippery-footed race. We slip when the roads are smooth. It is easy to go downhill, but it is not easy to do so without falling.

Sorrow, a quarrel with God: You remember the Quaker saying to the lady who was wearing mourning garments years after one of her children had died, "Madam, have you not forgiven God yet?" There is a truth about that remark. Some people do not forgive God for what He has done. Their sorrow amounts to them having a quarrel with God over how He does things.

Sorrow sinks us low: The nautilus, when disturbed, folds up its sails and sinks into the depths, and even so in every hour of storm, we descend into the depths of divine love.

Sorrow soothed: You had a little medicine to give your boy the other night, and it had a bad flavor, but you mixed it with some sweet dessert and he never tasted the bitterness. In the same way, the pangs of separation will be mixed up with the sweetness of seeing Christ so that you will not mourn.

Souls, care for: A ship was crossing the Atlantic the other day, and it came across that disabled emigrant ship, the *Denmark*. Suppose the captain had kept on his course. He could have looked another way and resolved not to be detained. He might have argued, "I am bound to do the best for my owners. It will hinder me greatly if I go messing around after this vessel. I had better go by and not see it, or I can hurry to the port and send out help." It could have been done, and nobody would have been the wiser, for the ship would have gone down soon. The captain of that vessel was a man of nobler breed. He did not hide himself nor turn a blind eye toward the vessel in distress.

What did the captain do? All honor to him, he came near and took the ship in tow. This was not all. He discovered that she could not keep afloat, so he resolved to take those hundreds of emigrants on board his own ship. But he could not carry them and his cargo too. What then? The decision was greatly to his honor. The cargo was thrown overboard. God's blessing rests on that man. The freight went into the sea, and the passengers were taken on board and carried to the nearest port. He could have easily hidden himself. So could you, you Christian people, as you call yourselves. Can you go through this world and always have a blind eye to the case of lost sinners?

Soul-winning: I knew someone who used to have a man call upon him in the way of business and bring certain articles that he bought across the counter. This tradesman said one day to himself, "I have dealt with that man for nine or ten years, and we have hardly passed the time of day. He has brought in his work, and I have paid him across the counter, but I have never tried to do him any good. Surely this cannot be right. Providence has put him in my way, and I should at least have asked him whether he is saved in Christ."

Well, the next time the man came, our good brother's spirit failed him, and he did not attempt to begin a religious conversation. The man never came again, but a boy brought in the next lot of goods. "What are you doing here?" asked the shopkeeper.

"Father is dead," said the boy.

My friend, the shopkeeper, said to me, "I could never forgive myself. I could not stay in the shop that day. I felt that I was guilty of that man's blood, but I had not thought of it before. How can I ever clear myself from the guilty fact that when I did think of it, my ungracious fear and hesitation prevented me from opening my mouth?"

My own dear friends and companions, do not bring upon yourselves such bitter regrets! Avoid them by daily watching to save people from the second death.

Soul-winning: When a sportsman goes hunting after game, he does not know which way he will go, nor does he commit himself in that matter. If he is stalking deer, he may have to go up the mountainside, down the glen, across the stream, or away among the heather. Where his sport leads him, he follows. It is the same with the genuine soul-winner. He leaves himself free to follow his one object. He does not know where he is going, but he does know what he is going after. He expends himself to win souls for Jesus. On the railway, he speaks to anyone who happens to be in the same carriage. In the shop, he looks for opportunities to make a spiritual impression on a customer. He sows beside all waters and in all soils. He carries a loaded gun, ready to take aim at once. That is the person whom God is likely to bless.

Speaking evil of Christ: When a person speaks against the Lord Jesus, I generally find that if you follow him home, he would rather not have you go inside for fear that his inner life would be known. He does not want you to see the skeleton in the closet. I have so often met with this fact in actual life that when I have heard a man speak bitterly of my Master, I have formed my opinion and have not been wrong. A little inquiry has revealed so much that I have said, "It is not at all surprising that such a man would speak evil of Christ. It is as natural for such a man to talk against Christ as for a dog to bark." When a bad fellow once praised Socrates, that philosopher said, "I wonder what I can have been doing wrong that such a man would speak well of me." If lustful lips praised the Savior, one might begin to be afraid; but when they denounce and ridicule Him, we feel that it is the only tribute that sin can pay to purity.

Spiritual change: The change that we have seen in some people has been as complete as that which could have been brought about by that fabled mill into which, the legend says, they put old men, turned the handle, and turned them out as young men again. Truly, a far greater renovation is worked in mind and heart where Jesus comes. People are *blessed in him* (Psalm 72:17).

Spiritual life: Just as certain insects take their color from the leaves they feed upon, so we have become dyed to the core of our nature with the living and incorruptible Word, which has proved its own inspiration by inspiring us with its spirit. We now live in the Word as the fish lives in the stream; it is the element of our spiritual life.

Spiritual life: Visit often those hills of holiness where the atmosphere is stimulating for your newborn spirit. I notice how people who are sickly will leave their homes and journey far for health. Not only will they sojourn upon the sunny shore of the Mediterranean, but they will encounter the merciless cold of the Alps in the middle of winter at St. Maritz or Davoust in the hope of restoration. If physicians would only guarantee lengthening of life, people would emigrate to inhospitable Siberia or banish themselves to Greenland's icy mountains. People will do anything for life. Will we not, then, be desirous to do all that we can to nourish our spiritual life? Christians, do not do anything that will damage your heaven-born lives. Act in this according to the highest prudence.

Spiritual life neglected: The other day we read in the newspapers of two people in America who were found dead from starvation and cold, and we also read that each of these people had a considerable sum of money. We say, "What fools!" People with much money on them or hidden away in their rooms, yet suffering the adversities of need until they actually die of hunger! What insanity this is! Yet are those more sane who harm and suppress their spiritual life for the sake of intellectual pride, carnal joy, or the esteem of men? Is not the spirit infinitely more precious than the body? Brethren, if we starve at all, let us starve our bodies and not our spirits. If anything must be suppressed, let it be the lower nature. Let us not live eagerly for this world and halfheartedly for the world to come. Having the divine life within us, let us not neglect to feed it and supply its needs.

Spiritually in tune: Before the song leader begins, we sometimes hear his tuning fork. He is getting the keynote into his ear. When he comes forward, he often sounds that tuning fork before he begins to sing. That is what David does. He sounds the tuning fork with this clear note, *Bless the Lord, O my soul* (Psalm 103:1). It is good for everyone to be ready to sing harmoniously. It is a pity when those who gather to worship do not know what they are doing. I wish I could always have you spiritually in tune and keep in tune myself. I fear we are often half a note too flat. The words before us are the keynote of this psalm, and all the music is set to it and closes with it, as if to show that praise is the alpha and omega of a Christian life. Praise is the life of life. So we begin, so we continue, and so will we end, *world without end* (Ephesians 3:21).

Stand fast: Some time ago, there was a ship outside a certain harbor. A heavy sea made the ship roll fearfully. A dense fog blotted out all buoys and lights. The captain had never left the wheel. He could not tell his way into the harbor, and no pilot could get out to him for a long time. Eager passengers urged him to be courageous and make a dash for the harbor. He said, "No. It is not my duty to run such a great risk. A pilot is required here, and I will wait for one if I have to wait a week."

The truest courage is that which can bear to be accused of cowardice. When you cannot hear the foghorn and have no pilot, it is much wiser to wait than to steam on and wreck your ship on the rocks. Our wise captain waited his time, and at last he saw the pilot's boat coming to him over the churning sea. When the pilot was at his work, the captain's anxious wait was over. The church is like that ship. She is pitched to and fro in the storm and the dark, and the Pilot has not yet come. The weather is very threatening. All around, the darkness hangs like a stormy cloud. Before long, though, Jesus will come walking on the water. He will bring us safe to the desired haven. Let us wait with patience. Stand fast! Stand fast! Jesus is coming, and in Him is our sure hope.

Starving souls: The experiment of the Frenchman who had just brought his horse to live on a straw a day when it died is being repeated among us. Faith is literally being starved to death. What a poor diet some people prescribe for their souls! They do not even smell at marrow and fatness!

Steadfastness: In the old Roman days, when a sentry was placed in his position by a centurion, he never thought of leaving his post. Rocks might roam, but not sentinels of the Empire. Among the ashes in Pompeii was found a sentry standing in his place with the javelin in his hand. He had not flinched amid the deadly shower that fell from the volcano and buried the city. His centurion, in the name of the emperor, had placed him there, and there he stood. How steadfast and immovable should they be whom the Lord Himself has set in their place in connection with His church!

"Stick to your last": The proverb says, "Stick to your shoe form, cobbler," and I would say, "Stick to your pulpit, minister." Stick to your work, and you will find quite enough for all the strength you have, and even more. Oh, for preachers who *shall never hold their peace* (Isaiah 62:6)!

Storms in life: Remember, there are days in every life voyage in which the storms of life puts all human power to the test. Even in the fairest weather, we are all too inclined to run onto rocks or quicksand, but the voyage of life is seldom an entirely pleasant one, and we must be prepared for storms. Our own unaided strength will not endure the waves and the winds of the ocean of life, and if you are trusting to yourself, the result will be disaster.

Strength in touching God: We are to be like that fabled giant whom Hercules could not overcome for a long while because he was a child of the earth, and every time he was thrown down, he touched his mother earth and rose with fresh strength. Hercules had to hold him overhead in his arms and then strangle him. Whenever you are thrown down and touch God in your faintness and weakness, you will find that He restores your soul (Psalm 23:3). *To them that have no might he increaseth strength* (Isaiah 40:29).

Striking testimony: One of our evangelists wrote to me that when he was praying with an inquirer and trying to lead him to Jesus, he was much helped by a working man who came in, knelt down by their side, and said, "Lord Jesus, save this poor soul, even as You saved me at two o'clock this morning." Somehow that "two o'clock" greatly helped the inquirer, putting such a reality into the transaction. He thought, "This man knows he was saved at two o'clock in the morning; why should I not be saved now at eight o'clock in the evening?" I do not say that we can all tell the date of our conversion; many of us cannot. But if we can throw in such details, let us do so, for they help to make our testimony powerful.

Subservience, dishonorable: It was the custom with certain Oriental tyrants to require ambassadors of foreign powers to lie in the dust before them. Some Europeans, for the sake of trade interests, submitted to the degrading ceremony; but when it was demanded of the representative of England, he refused to lower his country in that way. God forbid that he who speaks for God would dishonor the King of kings by a pliant submission.

Success of the simple gospel: Proclaim the simple gospel. The more you tell about forgiveness bought with blood, the better. I saw our dear brother Archibald G. Brown, and he told me of a poor fellow in East London who had been visited by a soul-winning brother. He had been a wild and wicked man. He was sick, and the visitor talked long with him. It seemed to make no impression, until one day he explained substitution to him. The man asked directly, "If I believe in Jesus, are you telling me that He took all my sins upon Himself?"

"Yes, He bore all your sins in His own body on the tree."

"Well, well," the man exclaimed, "if He took them, then I do not have them?"

"No," said the other man. "That is the glorious truth. The Lord suffered for your sins."

"Then I will not have to suffer for them?"

"No," said the visitor. "Your sin is put away."

"I never heard that before," said the rough man. "That is the most wonderful thing I ever heard. I believe it. Blessed be God. I believe it. I am saved."

Soon after, his son came in, and the visitor began exhorting him. The older man cried out, "Give him that little bit; that will do it." Just so, that little bit will do it. The visitor told the story of the Lord Jesus dying in the sinner's place, and the little bit did the work. Our main business should be to cry, *Behold the Lamb of God, which taketh away the sin of the world* (John 1:29).

Suffering saints: Sufferers are our teachers. They educate us for the skies. When people of God can suffer, when they can bear poverty, bereavement, or sickness, and still rejoice in God, we learn the way to live the higher and more Christly life. After Patrick Hamilton had been burned in Scotland, someone said to his persecutors, "If you are going to burn any more people, you had better do it in a cellar, for the smoke of Hamilton's burning has opened the eyes of hundreds." It was always so. Suffering saints are living seed.

Suffering, yet shining: See how the storm sweeps around that light out there, set up in mid-ocean on the Eddystone rock. The waters leap over it, threatening to put out its flame, but will the light complain? Standing where it is, beaten by Atlantic billows and braving the full fury of the storm, it is doing more good than if it were set up in Hyde Park for lords and ladies to look at. The persecuted saint occupies a place where he warns and enlightens, and therefore suffers.

Sun of Righteousness: Many of the wise men of the period should be treated as Diogenes treated Alexander. The conqueror of the world said to the man in the tub, "What can I do for you?" He thought he could do everything for the poor philosopher. Diogenes only replied, "Get out of the sunlight." These wise people cannot do us a greater favor than to remove their learned selves from standing between us and the sunlight of the ever-blessed gospel of the glory of Christ. These Alexanders may go on ruling the Christian world and the infidel world, but they have not conquered us, for our faith and joy lie outside the world in the Sun of Righteousness, whose light is the rejoicing of our eyes.

Sunset glories: I watched a glorious sunset, and I marveled at the beauty with which the evening skies were all ablaze and adoring Him who gave them their matchless coloring. I went to the same spot the next evening, hoping to be again enraptured with the gorgeous splendor of ending day, but there were no clouds, and therefore, no glories. It is true that the canopy of sapphire was there, but no magnificent array of clouds formed golden masses with edges of burning crimson. No islands of loveliest hue were set in a sea of emerald. There were no great blazes of splendor or flaming peaks of mountains of fire. The sun was as bright as before, but for lack of dark clouds on which to pour out its luster, its magnificence was unrevealed. A man who would live and die without trials would be like a setting sun without clouds.

Superfluities: You have seen a rose tree that perhaps was bearing very few roses, and you half wondered why. It was a good rose tree and was planted in good soil, but its flowers were few. You looked around it, and eventually you perceived that suckers were growing up from its roots. These suckers come from the old original briar on which the rose had been grafted, and this rose has a superfluity of strength that is used in these suckers. These superfluities, or overflows, took away from the rose the life that it required so that it could not produce the full number of flowers that you expected from it. There must be a removal of this excess in order that we may receive with meekness the engrafted Word that is able to save our souls (James 1:21).

Supplements of good: I acquire certain little expenses in connection with my study. We need a few wafers, which may be paid for out of petty cash, but I have never spent, as far as I remember, a single penny for string and brown paper because as a reader and writer, I buy books, and the string and brown paper are given to me. I purchase the books, but the string and brown paper come to me added as a routine matter. You are to spend your strength on the high and noble purpose of glorifying God, and then the minor matters of *What shall we eat? or, What shall we drink? or, Wherewithal shall we be clothed?* (Matthew 6:31) are thrown in as extras. Earthly things are merely brown paper and string, and I hope you never think too much of them. However, some people get so much of this brown paper and string that they glory in them and expect us to fall down and worship them.

Sympathy: I heard about a lady who was out in the snow one night and was so very cold that she cried out, "Oh, those poor people who have such little money, how little warmth they have, and how destitute they must be! I will send a hundred pounds of coal to twenty families at the least." However, when she reached her own house, there was a fine fire burning, and she sat there with her feet by the fire and enjoyed an excellent tea, and she said to herself, "Well, it is not very cold after all. I do not think that I will send that coal – at least not now."

The sufferer thinks of the sufferer, even as the poor help the poor. The divine wonder is that this Lord of ours, *though he was rich, yet for [our] sakes became poor* (2 Corinthians 8:9), now takes delight in helping the poor. Having been tempted, He helps the tempted (Hebrews 4:15). His own trials make Him desire to bless those who are tried.

Sympathy: It is greatly comforting to have a person with you who feels just as you feel – who, when you are sad, seems to be sad too, who worries when you worry, and sorrows in your sorrows. "Mother," said a little girl once, "I cannot understand. Mrs. Smith says I do her so much good. Poor Mrs. Smith has lost her husband, Mother, and she is very sad. She sits and cries, and I get up and lay my cheek on her cheek, and I cry and say that I love her, and then she says that I comfort her." That is indeed the truest form of consolation, is it not? *Weep with them that weep* (Romans 12:15). That is how God, my God, will hear me, understanding me and sympathizing with me.

Sympathy: There is a legend connected with Rufus and Alexander. I have never read it, but I have seen it depicted in glowing colors by an artist in a cathedral in Belgium. I saw a series of paintings that represented Christ bearing His cross through the streets of Jerusalem, and among the crowd, the artist placed a countryman looking on, carrying with him his mattock and spade as if he had just come into the town from laboring in the fields.

In the next picture, this countryman is evidently moved to tears by seeing the cruelties practiced upon the Redeemer, and he shows his sympathy so plainly that the cruel persecutors of our Lord, who are watching the spectators, observe it and gather angrily around him. The countryman's two boys, Alexander and Rufus, are there too. Rufus is the boy with the red hair. He is impassioned and confident, bold and outspoken, and you can see that one of the rough men has just been smacking him in the head for showing sympathy with the poor cross-bearing Savior.

The next picture represents the father taken and compelled to bear the cross, while Alexander holds his father's mattock and Rufus carries his father's spade, and they are going along close by the Lord Jesus, pitying Him greatly. If they cannot bear the cross, they will at least help their father by carrying the tools. Of course, it is only a legend, but who marvels if Alexander and Rufus saw their father carry Christ's cross so well so that they, too, would afterward count it in their glory to be followers of the Crucified One (Mark 15:21) – so that Paul should say when he wrote down the name of Rufus that he was a choice man, for so we may translate the passage, *chosen in the Lord* or "The choice one of the Lord" (Romans 16:13). He was a distinguished Christian with great depth of Christian experience, and in all respects, he was a fit descendant of a remarkable father and mother.

* * * *

- Safe walking can only come of careful walking.

- Saintly souls should not be lodged in filthy bodies.

- Sanctified adversity enlivens our spiritual sensitiveness.

- Saving faith is a lifelong act.

- Show religion is a vain show.

- Sick saints are set to take the night watches.

- Simple trust and grateful service make a link more precious than gold.

- Sin in silk is as great a rebel as sin in rags.

- Sin may drive you from Sinai; it should draw you to Calvary.

- Some saints can be led with a thread of hair.

- Some soil needs even cross-plowing and scarifying.

- Sorrow unsettles the judgment.

- Soul music is the soul of music.

- Strong faith is always on the winning side.

- Style the reprobate an angel of light, and he is nonetheless a devil.

- Sympathy in sin is conspiracy in crime.

Talents, to be used: A tradesman who is prospering seldom has much money to show; it is all needed in his business. Sometimes he can hardly put his hand on a ten-dollar bill because his cash is all being used. His golden grain is all sown in the field of his trade. Speaking for myself, I cannot find any room for glorying in myself, for if I have either grace or strength, I certainly have none to spare. I have barely enough for the work in hand and not enough for the service that lies ahead. Our talent is not to be hung on our watch chain, but is to be traded with.

Temptations everywhere: People who live in London do not need to go across the street to meet the devil. The very atmosphere of a great city is close and hot with the stench of sin. As flies in summer will torment you, so temptations will torment you no matter where you may go. People of business, you do not need to ask for temptations. They are abundant in every trade. They multiply like gnats. They swarm in the factory, the accountant's office, the stock exchange, and the shop. The Christian in public does not need to wish for temptations, for they will not be ashamed to approach him in the open streets.

This age tests the backbone of every Christian. A man needs to be a man at such an hour as this. We must not be spiritually immature or weak now. We have come into the very heart of the fight, and woe to that man who cannot endure temptation; but blessed is the man who can bear it even to the end.

Testimony, personal: I was quite surprised the other day when a carriage driver said to me, "You believe that the Lord directs the way of His people, don't you, sir?"

I said, "Yes, I do. Do you know anything about it?"

"Why, yes" he said. "This morning I was praying for the Lord to direct my way, and you got in my carriage, and I felt that it was a good beginning for the day."

We then began talking about the things of God. That carriage driver should not have been the first to speak about the things of God. As a minister of the gospel, I should have had the first word. We have much to blame ourselves for in this respect. We hold our tongues because we do not know how a word might be received, but we might as well make the experiment. No harm could come of trying.

Suppose you were to go into a place where people were sick and dying, and you had medicine with you that would heal them. Would you not be eager to give them some of it? Would you say nothing about it because you did not know how it might be received? How could you know how it would be received unless you make the offer? Tell poor souls about Jesus. Tell them how His grace healed you, and perhaps they will answer, "You are the very person I need. You have brought me the news I have longed to hear."

Testing: We all need testing, do we not? Would you like to cross a railway bridge if you were told that it had never been tested by a train? When the first exhibition was built, I remember that they marched troops along the galleries to test them. Do you not desire to have your hope for eternity tested? The Lord draws near to us in ways that inspire our fears because He wants to test us. What is the result of the test? Do you not feel your own weakness? Does not this drive you to those who are strong for strength? You feel your own sinfulness, and you run to the Lord Jesus for righteousness. Testing has a useful, good effect in eliminating self-confidence and driving you to put your confidence where God wants it to rest.

The law, a mirror: The law is very useful because it shows us our defects and stains. It is like the mirror that a lady holds up to her face so that she may see if there is any spot on it. But she cannot wash her face with the mirror. When the mirror has done its best, the same stains remain. It cannot take away a single spot. It can only show where one is. And the law, although it reveals our sins, our shortcomings, and our transgressions, cannot remove the sin or the transgression. It is no good for that purpose because it was never intended to accomplish such a task.

The Lord, a sight of: When the Lord revealed Himself to that holy man, Mr. Walsh, he was compelled to cry, "Hold, Lord! Remember I am only an earthen vessel, and if I have more of this delight, I will die." Someone said he would like to die of that disease, and I am very much of his opinion. They say, "See Naples and die," but to improve on it, someone else said, "See Naples and live" – and truly, this is the better sight of the two. I would gladly see my Lord so as to live to His praise. Oh, for such a vision that would shape my life, my thought, and my whole being until I became like my Lord!

The Lord, a wall of fire: A Christian lady not long ago dreamed a dream that was not a dream, but was fact. She saw herself as surrounded with God – encircled above, beneath, and all around, as with a blaze of light. Brilliance inconceivable made a covering for her. While she stood in the midst of the glory, she saw all her cares, troubles, temptations, and sins wandering about the outside of the wall of light, unable to reach her. Unless that light itself would open and make a way for them, she was peacefully secure, although she could see the dangers that would otherwise destroy her. Is not the Lord *a wall of fire round about* us, and *the glory in the midst* (Zechariah 2:5)?

The poor can become nobility of heaven: There lies a poor girl in a loft where the stars look between the tiles and where the moon gleams on the ragged hangings of the mattress where she bravely suffers, and without complaining, gradually dissolves unto death. No matter how obscure and unknown she may be, she has been kept from the great transgression. Even though she was severely tempted, she has still held fast her purity and integrity. Her prayers, unheard by others, have gone up before the Lord, and she dies in the Lord, saved through Jesus Christ. No one will preach her funeral sermon, but she will not miss that voice from heaven saying, *Write, Blessed are the dead which die in the Lord* (Revelation 14:13).

The Word, a key: There was never a lack of soul trouble yet that did not have a key to open it in the Word of God. For our pain, here is a painkiller. For our darkness, here is a lamp. For our loneliness, here is a friend. It is like the garden of Eden: a double river of peace flows through it.

Trouble, God thanked for: I was reading today of old Mr. Dodd, who is a person the Puritans are always quoting. He is a man who did not write books, but he seems to have said things with which other people made their books attractive. It is said that this old Mr. Dodd had a great trouble, a bodily complaint I will not mention, but it is one of the most painful a man can suffer from. When he was told that this had come upon him, and that it was incurable, the old man shed a few natural tears at the great and excruciating pain, but eventually said, "This is evidently from God, and God never sent me anything that was not for my good; therefore, let us kneel down together and thank God for this." It was well said of the old man, and it was well done of him, that he thanked God most sincerely. Oh yes, let us kneel down together and thank God for our trouble!

Troubles: A Scottish saint said that when they met in the moss or by the hillside, and were harassed by Claverhouse and his men, Christ was present at the sacraments in the heather much more than He ever was afterward when they got into the church and sat down quietly. Our worst days are often our best days, and in the dark we see stars that we never saw in the light. So we will not care at all what it is that may happen to us here as long as God is with us and our faith in Him is genuine. Christian people, I am not going to sympathize with you, but I congratulate you upon your troubles, for the cross of Christ is precious.

Troubles met one by one: Take life and death just as they come, bit by bit. You know how the Spartans endeavored to keep back the Persians. They took possession of the pass of Thermopylae, and there the brave two hundred stood and held the way against multitudes. The enemy could only advance one by one. Do not think of all the armies of your troubles that are coming in the future, but meet them one by one. *Sufficient unto the day is the evil thereof* (Matthew 6:34).

Troubles, our glory: There is no glory in being a feather-bed soldier, a man adorned with a fancy uniform, but never decorated by a scar or dignified by a wound. All that you ever hear of such a soldier is that his spurs jingle on the pavement as he walks. There is no history for this carpet knight. He is just a peacock. He never smelled gunpowder in his life, or if he did, he brought out a smelling bottle to kill the offensive odor. Well, that will not make much of an impression in the story of nations. If we could have our choice, and if we were as wise as the Lord Himself, we would choose the troubles He has appointed us, and we would not spare ourselves a single pain.

Trust, childlike: A blind child was in his father's arms, and a stranger came into the room and took him right away from his father, yet he did not cry or complain. His father said to him, "Johnny, are you afraid? You do not know the person who is holding you."

"No, Father," he said. "I do not know who he is, but you do."

Trust, false: I have heard of someone who, on his deathbed, held bags of money to his heart, but he was forced to put them away and cry, "These will not do! These will not do!" It will be a sorry business if we have been trusting in our feelings, our charity, our patriotism, our courage, or our honesty. When we come to die, we will be made to feel that these cannot satisfy the claims of divine justice or give us a passport to the skies.

Trust in a living Savior: Some years ago, someone who wanted to mock our holy faith brought out a poster that was hung up everywhere. It asked, "Can you trust in a dead man?" Our answer would have been, "No, nobody can trust in a man who is dead!" However, those who printed the poster knew that they were misrepresenting our faith. Jesus is no longer dead. He rose again on the third day. We have certain and infallible proofs of it. It is a historical fact, better proved than almost any other fact that is commonly received as historical, that He did really rise again from the grave. He arose no more to die. He has gone out of the land of tears and death. He has gone to the region of immortality. He sits at the right hand of God, even the Father, and He reigns there forever. We love Him who died, but we rejoice that He who died is not dead, but *ever liveth to make intercession for* us (Hebrews 7:25).

Trust in Providence: I was going through these streets one day, driven by a friend in a four-wheeled coach, and he, being a good driver, had to drive into narrow places where it seemed to me we would be crushed by the wagons and omnibuses. I cringed in my timidity, and I expressed my unwise alarms so freely, that he laid the reins in my hand with a smile and said, "If you cannot trust me, would you like to drive yourself?" I was entirely free from that desire, and I assured him that he could drive as he liked rather than make me the charioteer. Surely the great God could well put the same proposal to those who are complaining of His providence. If we cannot trust Him, could we manage better ourselves?

Trust, simple: I once lived where my neighbor's garden was only divided from mine by a very imperfect hedge. My neighbor had a dog, and his dog was a shockingly bad gardener and did not improve my beds. So one evening, while I walked alone, I saw this dog doing some damage. Being a long way off, I threw a stick at him and gave him some earnest advice that he should go home. Instead of going home, the dog came to me with the stick in his mouth, wagging his tail. He dropped the stick at my feet and looked up at me most kindly. What could I do except pat him and call him a good dog and regret that I had ever spoken roughly to him? It brings tears to my eyes as I talk about it! The dog mastered me by his trust in me.

The illustration is to the point. If you will trust God as the dog trusted me, you will overcome. God will be held by your trust in such a way that He could not strike you, but must accept you for Jesus's sake. If you trust Him, you have the key of His heart, the key of His house, the key of His heaven. If you can trust your God in Jesus Christ, you have become a child of God. I see a philosophy in the choice of faith.

Truth: It is true that you have not perceived spiritual things, but that is no proof that there are none to perceive. The whole case is like that of the Irishman who tried to upset evidence by non-evidence. Four witnesses saw him commit a murder. He pleaded that he was not guilty, and he wanted to establish his innocence by producing forty people who did not see him do it. Of what use would that have been? If forty people declare that there is no power of the Holy Spirit going with the

Word, this only proves that the forty people do not know what others do know. If there are four of us who do know it, then we will not cease our witness. We receive God's Word as the word of God because it comes to us with that power which effectually works in those who believe (1 Thessalonians 2:13).

Truth, divinely applied: Before I came to London, a man met me one Sunday in a dreadful state of rage. He vowed that he would horsewhip me for bullying him from the pulpit. "What have I said?" I asked.

"What have you said? You looked me in the face, and said, 'What more can God do for you? Will He give you a good wife? You have had one. You have killed her by bad treatment. You have just got another wife, and you are likely to do the same by her.'"

"Well," I said, "did you kill your first wife by your bad treatment?"

"They say so; but I was married on Saturday," he said. "Did you not know it?"

"No, I did not, I assure you," I replied.

The cap fit him.

Truth, fidelity to the: As the Roman sentinel in Pompeii stood to his post even when the city was destroyed, so do I stand to the truth of the atonement even though the church is being buried beneath the boiling mud showers of modern heresy. Everything else can wait, but this one truth must be proclaimed with a voice of thunder. Others may preach as they will, but as for this pulpit, it will always resound with the substitution of Christ. *God forbid that I should glory, save in the cross of our Lord Jesus Christ* (Galatians 6:14). Some may continually preach Christ as an example, and others may perpetually talk about His coming to glory. We also preach both of these, but mainly we *preach Christ crucified*, which is *unto the Jews a stumblingblock, and unto the Greeks foolishness*; but unto them that are saved, *Christ the power of God, and the wisdom of God* (1 Corinthians 1:23-24).

Truth, spread of the: Dr. Valpy, the author of a great many textbooks, wrote the following simple lines as his confession of faith:

In peace let me resign my breath,
    And Thy salvation see;
My sins deserve eternal death,
    But Jesus died for me.

Valpy is dead and gone, but he gave those lines to dear old Dr. Marsh, the headmaster at Beckenham, who put them over his study mantel shelf. The Earl of Roden came in and read them. "Will you give me a copy of those lines?" asked the good earl.

"I will be glad to do so," said Dr. Marsh, and he copied them. Lord Roden took them home and put them over his mantel shelf. General Taylor, a Waterloo hero, came into the room and noticed them. He read them over and over again while staying with Earl Roden, until his Lordship remarked, "I say, friend Taylor, I would think you know those lines by heart."

He answered, "I do know them by heart; indeed, my very heart has grasped their meaning."

He was brought to Christ by that humble rhyme. General Taylor handed those lines to an officer in the army who was going out to the Crimean War. He came home to die, and when Dr. Marsh went to see him, the poor soul in his weakness said, "Good sir, do you know this verse that General Taylor gave to me? It brought me to my Savior, and I die in peace." To Dr. Marsh's surprise, he repeated the lines.

Only think of the good that four simple lines may do. All of you who know the healing power of the wounds of Jesus, be encouraged. Spread this truth in any way you can.

Truth, strong: When Mohammed began his enterprise, he announced that paradise was to be found beneath the shadow of swords, and numbers of brave men rushed to the battle. They swept everything before them and stained continents with blood. They carried the name of Allah and Mohammed over Asia and Northern Africa, and seemed intent on conquering Europe; yet the work done will not endure. The prophet and his caliphs did indeed strive and cry and cause their voices to be heard in the street, but Christ's system is the very reverse of that. His weapons are not carnal. Behold His battle-ax and weapons of war! Truth divinely strong, with no human force behind it except that of holiness and love, a gospel full of gentleness and mercy to men, proclaimed not by the silver trumpets of kings, but by the plain voices of lowly men.

Truth, very personal: A man went out of this place one evening who was spoken to by one of our friends who happened to know him in trade and had a good opinion of him. "What! Have you been to hear our minister tonight?"

The good man answered, "Yes, I am sorry to say I have."

Our friend asked, "Why are you sorry?"

"Because," he said, "he has turned me inside out and spoiled my idea of myself. When I went into the Tabernacle, I thought I was the best man in Newington, but now I feel that my righteousness is worthless."

"Oh," said the friend, "that is all right. You will come again, I am sure. The Word has come home to you and has shown you the truth. You will get comfort soon."

That friend did come again, and he now takes pleasure in that very truth that turned him inside out. Now he comes on purpose so that the Word of the Lord may search him, try him, and be to him as a refiner's fire.

* * * *

- Take Christ to be the sole Savior of your soul.

- Take no rest from prayer, and give Him no rest.

- Temporal things are as the mirage in the desert.

- The accent of conviction is indispensable if you want to convince.

- The approval of God is more than the admiration of nations.

- The arrows of calamity are aimed at your sins.

- The believer has enduring reasons for enduring comfort.

- The Bible in the memory is better than the Bible in the bookcase.

- The Bible is the treasury of heavenly knowledge, the encyclopedia of divine science.

- The Bible is, to many people, God's *unopened* letter.

- The blank of nothingness did not stand in God's way when He came to create.

- The constable of the Tower of London stands in relationship to it and is concerned for its preservation. The Lord is not only the keeper and guarantor of my mercy, but He is the God of it.

- The cross is the last argument of God.

- The cure for vain glory is true glory.

- The devil's bread is all bran.

- The divine blesses the human, or the human could not bless the divine.

- The door of repentance opens into the halls of joy.

- The doorstep of the palace of wisdom is a humble sense of ignorance.

- The good Bible student has lips like a springing well.

- The great loaves of wisdom must be broken and crumbled into a bowl of milk for the children.

- The high road of truth to the heart runs through the ear.

- The *ipse dixit* (He said it Himself) of the Son of God suffices us.

- The lance with which we reach the hearts of men is that same lance that pierced the Savior's heart.

- The line of truth is as narrow as a razor's edge.

- The little things of God are more precious than the great things of man.

- The Lord gives unlimited credit at the Bank of Faith.

- The Lord is never voiceless except to the earless soul.

- The Lord loves adverbs as much as adjectives.

- The Lord loves to use tools that are not rusted with self-conceit.

- The mercy seat is no place for the demonstration of your abilities.

- The novelties of modern thought are a Dead Sea, but our gospel is an ocean of living water.

- The path to heaven lies by the dens of the leopards and the habitat of the young lions.

- The privileges of the gospel are the stumbling blocks of legalists.

- The stench of sin destroys the sweet odors of this world.

- The real eloquence of prayer is a believing desire.

- The safest truth is the simplest.

- The simple gospel that saves sinners also feeds saints.

- The star of today will be the sun of tomorrow.

- The thing we glory in, even if it is a dear child, may turn out to be a whip for our backs – a Cain and not a consolation.

- The treasury of heaven lies open to faith.

- There is a November of fogs in the year of most people.

- There is music without words, and there is prayer without words.

- There is no hewing stones without hard strikes.

- There is no monotony in real joy.

- There is no sin-killer like the Word of God.

- There is something to be made out of a man who has enough stuff in him to be opposed to the gospel. A good sword will make a good plowshare. God can make apostles out of persecutors.

- Think well of Him who thinks so graciously of you.

- To do right is better than to prosper.

- True religion is no new thing.

- Trust in the precious blood; that is the great sin-killer.

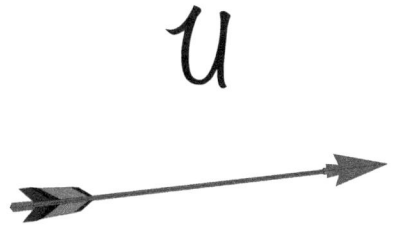

Untried faith, questionable faith: We cannot say we are blessed until our graces have been tried and proved; but when they have been tried and proved, and we have endured the test in God's great testing house, then we are blessed, and not until then. There is a man who has received a stack of what appear to be banknotes, and he thinks he is very rich. Have you tried to pass one of them? Have you taken one of them to a bank? No, poor fool! He does not want to have his fine fortune tried. He is angry when you suggest any doubt, yet his wealth is mere fiction. Those banknotes are banknotes of the Bank of Elegance, and if he were to attempt to pass them, he might rather be suspected to be a thief than be judged to be a rich man.

Much faith in this world is no better than that; and he is not blessed, but blinded, who possesses it. He is blessed who has tried his faith, who has gone to God with a promise and has received an answer to his prayer. He is blessed who has had his faith tried, who, having been put into the furnace, has by that faith in God been made to walk safely amid the flaming coals and has come out unharmed. Untried faith is questionable faith. Is it faith at all? Was there ever in this world a believer who was entirely without trouble, or a grain of faith that had undergone no trial?

Vessel of the church: The vessel of the church can never be wrecked. She rocks and reels in the fierce storm, but she is sound from stem to stern, and her Pilot steers her with a hand omnipotently wise. Her bow is in the wave, but she divides the sea and shakes off the mountainous waves as a lion shakes the dew from his mane! Fiercer storms than those of the present have beat upon her, yet she has kept her head to the wind, and in the very teeth of hell's tremendous tempests, she has plowed her glorious way; and she will continue to do so until she reaches her appointed haven.

Waiting is service: Have you not sometimes seen the telegraph boys standing or sitting still at the post office when there is no message to be delivered? They are as much doing their work by waiting as when they are delivering a message. In waiting, they serve; and in the same way, they most truly serve the Lord who give up all idea of pleasing themselves, and who go or stay as best pleases Him to whom they willingly offer themselves to be His servants.

Walk of faith: It is nothing for a man to walk down here upon the ground. However, to walk up high upon a slender thread that the eye can hardly see is a feat of skill at which people gaze with admiration, and to walk on what the eye cannot see at all, or that the foot cannot feel, needs an even higher skill. Such is the walk of faith.

Water carriers for others who are thirsty: I remember sitting one day in an inn at Cologne, looking out of a window upon a square. There was not much to see. I saw what there was to see as I occasionally looked up from my writing. I saw a man coming to a pump that stood in the middle of the square, and from that pump he filled a vessel. A little while later, I saw the same man again filling his buckets. All that morning I saw no one else except that one water-loving individual, filling his buckets again and again. I thought to myself, what can he be? He is always drawing water. Then I perceived that he was a water carrier, someone who carried water to families in the adjoining streets. He might well come often to the fountain himself since he was supplying others. You who are water carriers for thirsty souls must necessarily come often to the well yourselves, and be thankful that your Master is always willing to meet you and give you rich supplies.

Way to heaven is uphill: I saw a good man taking it easy the other day. He was riding on a bicycle with both feet off the pedals and with the brake in full force. I did not blame the cyclist, but one thing was quite clear: he was going down the hill. He would not have had his feet upon the rests in that manner if he had been going uphill. Whenever you begin to put your legs up and have no more work to do, you are going downhill, and there is no doubt about it. The way to heaven is uphill, and every inch of the way requires effort, for *the kingdom of heaven suffereth violence* (Matthew 11:12).

Weak-minded people can be saved: A young man who had fallen into sin came to me in deep despair of mind. He was so despondent that his very face bore witness to his misery. He had the appearance of one who could not live much longer as he was. I had tried to set the gospel clearly before him on the previous Lord's Day, but he told me that he could not grasp it because by his sin he had reduced his mind to such a state that he felt himself to be little better than a fool. He was not speaking nonsense, either, for there are sins that destroy the intellect.

I told him that Jesus Christ could save those who are weak-minded – that even if his mind, in part, was impaired as the result of sin, yet there was quite enough mind left to be made glad with a sense of forgiveness since there was more than enough to make him heavy with a sense of guilt. I encouraged that brother as best I could, but I could not bring about any change by my own efforts. Soon the Lord Jesus Christ came to him, and he is now a happy, earnest, joyful Christian. Not long ago he sent an offering of thanksgiving to God for having lifted him up from the deeps he had fallen into. I hope there is a long life of real usefulness before him.

Wealth, unknown: We have heard of people in Australia who walked habitually over nuggets of gold. We have heard of a bridge being built with what seemed to be common stone, but it contained masses of golden ore. People did not know their wealth. Is it not a pity that you would be poor in comfort, yet have all the gold of consolation at your feet? Lying within your Bible leaves, you have checks for millions, yet you have barely a penny to spend.

Wholeheartedness: I have seen boys swimming in a river in the morning. One of them has just dipped his toes in the water, and he cries out as he shivers, "Oh, it's so cold!" Another has gone in up to his ankles, and he also declares it is very cold. But another boy dives in from the bank and rises in joy. All his blood is circulating, and he cries, "This is great! What a fine morning! The water is splendid!" That is the boy for enjoying a bath.

You Christian people who are paddling about in the shallow part of the Christian religion, just dipping your toes into it – you stand shivering in the cold air of the world that you are afraid to leave. Oh, that you would plunge into the river of life! How it would awaken and energize you! What spirit it would give you! Get all in, young man, get all in! Be a Christian fully and wholeheartedly. Serve the Lord with your whole being. Give yourself wholly to Him who bought you with His blood. Plunge into the sacred blood by grace, and you will exclaim with George Bubier:

> Oh, this is life! Oh, this is joy,
> My God, to find Thee so;
> Thy face to see, Thy voice to hear,
> And all Thy love to know.

"Why me?": I once had a dear friend, a man of God who is now in heaven, a clergyman of the Church of England, whose name was Curme. With a pleasant smile, he used to divide his name into two syllables, and say, "Cur me," which in Latin means, "Why me?"

> Why was I made to hear Thy voice,
> And enter while there's room;
> When thousands make a wretched choice,
> And rather starve than come?
> —Isaac Watts

Willing surrender: I think that it is much the same with our gift of ourselves to Christ and His people as it is with plucking a peach: if it is handled much, or is pulled off the tree by a rough hand, the beautiful bloom is quickly gone from it. Christ loves to have our hearts with the bloom on them. He delights to see us willingly yield ourselves.

Winning souls, desire for: Be on the lookout for new ways of serving the Master. As African travelers each now seem very eager to be the first to make a treaty with certain chieftains so that their territory may be annexed to this country or that, so seek to win new conquests for Christ and attach people to His cause before they are hopelessly lost to the devil.

Winning souls, wisdom needed: A gentleman who joined this church some time ago had been an atheist for years. In conversing with him, I learned that he had been educated at one of our great public schools, and he traced his unbelief to that fact. He said that on Sundays the boys were placed in a lofty gallery at the far end of a church where they could hardly hear a word that the clergyman said, but they simply sat imprisoned in a place where it was very hot in summer and cold in winter. On Sundays there were prayers, prayers, and prayers, but nothing that ever touched his heart, until he was so sick of prayers that he vowed if he once got out of the school, he would have nothing to do with religion. This is a sad result, but it is a frequent one. You Sunday school teachers can make your classes so boring to the children that they will hate Sunday. You can waste away the time in school without bringing the boys and girls to Christ, and so you may do more harm than good.

Wishes made prayers: It will be our wisdom to turn our kind wishes into prayers. Wishes are lame, but prayer has legs. Yes, it has wings with which it runs and even flies toward God. Wishes are baskets, but prayer fills them with bread. Wishes are clouds, but prayer is the rain.

Word, power of the: It was a pleasure to me in years past to enjoy the friendship of Mr. Brownlow North. Before conversion, he was a thorough man of the world, and I suppose he was about as frivolous and depraved as men of his position and character often are. After his conversion, he began to preach the gospel with great fervor, and certain of his old companions were full of spite against him, probably considering him to be a hypocrite.

One day when he was about to address a large congregation, a stranger handed him a letter, saying, "Read that before you preach." This letter contained a statement of certain faults of conduct committed by Brownlow North, and it ended with words to this effect: "How dare you, being conscious of the truth of all the above, pray and speak to the people this evening when you are such a vile sinner?"

The preacher put the letter into his pocket, entered the pulpit, and after prayer and praise, began his address to a very crowded congregation. However, before speaking on his text, he produced the letter and informed the people of its contents. Then he added, "All that is said in this letter is true, and it is a correct picture of the depraved sinner that I once was. But oh, how wonderful must the grace be that could awaken and raise me up from such a death in trespasses and sins, and make me what I appear before you tonight – a vessel of mercy, one who knows that all his past sins have been cleansed away through the atoning blood of the Lamb of God! It is about His redeeming love that I have now to tell you, and to plead with any here who are not yet reconciled to God to come this night in faith to Jesus so that He may take their sins away and heal them." Thus, instead of closing the preacher's mouth by this letter, the Enemy's attempt only opened the hearts of the people, and the Word was proclaimed with power.

Work, man's inferior to God's: Bring me a needle. This is a highly polished needle. What an instance of human skill to make such a small implement so bright and smooth. Bring me that microscope. I have just now put the wing of a butterfly under it. That is God's work, and as I enlarge it, I discover no imperfection, but more and more of marvelous beauty. That butterfly's wing under the microscope becomes wonderful, and I worship God as I gaze upon His handiwork. Take the butterfly away now and put your own needle in its place. Why, this is a rough bar of iron that has never been smoothed or polished. This is wretched workmanship. It does not seem right for delicate work. Such is all that man can make, even the best of it.

Workmen, joyful: Get a man at work at a statue – an artist whose whole soul is in his chisel, who knows that there is a bright spirit within that block of marble, and who intends to chip off all that hides the lovely image from his sight. See how he works! No one does anything well who does it sorrowfully. The best work that can be done is done by the happy, joyful workman; and so it is with Christ. He does not save souls because He has to, as though He would rather do something else if He could, but His very heart is in it. He rejoices to do it, and therefore He does it completely, and He communicates His joy to us as He does it.

Worldlings, their ambitions: A country scene passed under my own eye only a few hours ago. I sat by the stream, at a point where abundant springs poured forth new streams. It was a brook that was wide but shallow, and the pure water glided along refreshingly under the over-hanging boughs. Little children were there wading into the stream and enjoying its cool waters. One of them was a true representative of your wealthy merchants. He went fishing with a bright green glass bottle, and his ventures were successful. Again and again I heard his voice ring out most joyously and impressively: "Look! Look! Here! Here! Such a big 'un. I have caught such a big 'un!" It was by no means a whale that he had taken, but a fish that might be half an inch long. Yet how he exulted! "Such a big 'un!" To him the affairs of nations were as nothing compared with the great treasure he had taken.

This is like the gentleman at the stock exchange who has made that successful speculation. For the next few days, he will astonish every-body as they hear that it was "such a big 'un!" Earth, heaven, and hell, time and eternity, may all accept the cold shoulder now that the glass bottle contains its prey. I confess I was not carried away with admira-tion for the child's fortune, but neither did I envy him the fullness of his satisfaction.

His brother, not far off, varied my picture for me. He was less richly endowed, yet he had a very functional tin can with which he fished most diligently. Soon I heard his voice pitched in another key: "Nasty little things! They won't come here! I can't catch 'em! They are good for nothing! I won't try anymore." Then the impetuous genius threw his tin can with a splash into the water, and his enterprise was ended. That is the gentleman whose company has been liquidated, or whose goods will not command the market. Things will not come his way. He cannot find success. He has made a failure of it, and the news is in the *Gazette*. All society is out of order, or he would have certainly succeeded. He is sick of it all for the present.

You smile at my boys, but you people of the world, these are yourselves! You are those children, and your ambitions are the tiny fish. As Isaac Watts wrote,

> O happy man that lives on high,
>> While men lie grovelling here.

Without God, you are paddling in the brook of life, fishing for minnows.

Worldly pleasure, distasteful: If I had to sit in some people's company and hear what they talk about, it would be hell to me. One night, having to preach up in the north of England, this unfortunate circumstance occurred to me. When I got down to the railway, I was put into a first-class carriage with five sporting men who were going to the Doncaster races. Fortunately, they did not know me, but from the beginning to the end of their journey, their conversation was adorned with expressions that tortured me, and at last they fell on a subject that was unutterably loathsome.

I pray God that I may not be condemned to live with such people forever, for it would be hell to me. Ladies and gentlemen, you do not need to think that I rob myself of any pleasures when I do not go to racetracks or associate with the corrupt and immoral. It is my pleasure to keep far from the pleasures of those men whom I was forced to accompany. The pleasures of this world are so full of dust, dirt, and grit that he who has once washed his mouth clean of them declines another meal of such filth. You will lose no pleasure if you come to Christ.

World's attraction: You have heard of him who one day was speaking eloquently about philosophy to a crowd who greatly applauded him. He thought he had made many disciples, but suddenly the market bell rang, and not a single person remained. Gain was to be made, and in their opinion no philosophy could be compared to personal profit. They were hearers until the market bell rang, and then, as they had been hearers only, they stopped hearing also. I fear it is the same with our preaching. If the devil rings the bell for sin, for pleasure, for worldly amusement, or for evil gain, our admirers quickly leave us. The voice of the world drowns the voice of the Word.

* * * *

- Weak faith is a great fabricator of fears.
- We could do with less paint if we had more power.
- We need faith in every step of a holy life.
- We need less varnish and more verity.
- We need workshop faith as well as prayer-meeting faith.
- We act like a man today and a mouse tomorrow.
- We will not be muzzled like dogs, either to please the world or its master.
- When the devil is not troubled by us, he does not trouble us.
- When the Lord's black horses call at our door, they bring us double loads of blessing.
- When you are out for a holiday, be holy.
- Who wants to paddle around in a duck pond all his life? Launch out into the deep.
- Willful ignorance will bring terrible damnation.
- Wolves leap into the fold no matter how carefully you watch the door.
- Would you yoke an ant with an angel? If you did, they would be a far more equal pair than Christ and self.
- You cannot get an amount of conversions like you can an amount of steel pens.

- You have the milk of faith, but God wants you to have the cream of assurance.

- You lose the leverage of power if you fail in holiness.

- You may wash sin in cologne, but it does not smell any sweeter.

- Your father's kisses will make you forget your brother's frowns.

CHARLES H. SPURGEON
– A BRIEF BIOGRAPHY

C harles Haddon Spurgeon was born on June 19, 1834, in Kelvedon, Essex, England. He was one of seventeen children in his family (nine of whom died in infancy). His father and grandfather were Nonconformist ministers in England. Due to economic difficulties, eighteen-month-old Charles was sent to live with his grandfather, who helped teach Charles the ways of God. Later in life, Charles remembered looking at the pictures in *Pilgrim's Progress* and in *Foxe's Book of Martyrs* as a young boy.

Charles did not have much of a formal education and never went to college. He read much throughout his life though, especially books by Puritan authors.

Even with godly parents and grandparents, young Charles resisted giving in to God. It was not until he was fifteen years old that he was born again. He was on his way to his usual church, but when a heavy snowstorm prevented him from getting there, he turned in at a little

Primitive Methodist chapel. Though there were only about fifteen people in attendance, the preacher spoke from Isaiah 45:22: *Look unto me, and be ye saved, all the ends of the earth.* Charles Spurgeon's eyes were opened and the Lord converted his soul.

He began attending a Baptist church and teaching Sunday school. He soon preached his first sermon, and then when he was sixteen years old, he became the pastor of a small Baptist church in Cambridge. The church soon grew to over four hundred people, and Charles Spurgeon, at the age of nineteen, moved on to become the pastor of the New Park Street Church in London. The church grew from a few hundred attenders to a few thousand. They built an addition to the church, but still needed more room to accommodate the congregation. The Metropolitan Tabernacle was built in London in 1861, seating more than 5,000 people. Pastor Spurgeon preached the simple message of the cross, and thereby attracted many people who wanted to hear God's Word preached in the power of the Holy Spirit.

On January 9, 1856, Charles married Susannah Thompson. They had twin boys, Charles and Thomas. Charles and Susannah loved each other deeply, even amidst the difficulties and troubles that they faced in life, including health problems. They helped each other spiritually, and often together read the writings of Jonathan Edwards, Richard Baxter, and other Puritan writers.

Charles Spurgeon was a friend of all Christians, but he stood firmly on the Scriptures, and it didn't please all who heard him. Spurgeon believed in and preached on the sovereignty of God, heaven and hell, repentance, revival, holiness, salvation through Jesus Christ alone, and the infallibility and necessity of the Word of God. He spoke against worldliness and hypocrisy among Christians, and against Roman Catholicism, ritualism, and modernism.

One of the biggest controversies in his life was known as the "Down-Grade Controversy." Charles Spurgeon believed that some pastors of his time were "down-grading" the faith by compromising with the world or the new ideas of the age. He said that some pastors were denying the inspiration of the Bible, salvation by faith alone, and the truth of the Bible in other areas, such as creation. Many pastors who believed what Spurgeon condemned were not happy about this, and Spurgeon eventually resigned from the Baptist Union.

Despite some difficulties, Spurgeon became known as the "Prince of Preachers." He opposed slavery, started a pastors' college, opened an orphanage, led in helping feed and clothe the poor, had a book fund for pastors who could not afford books, and more.

Charles Spurgeon remains one of the most published preachers in history. His sermons were printed each week (even in the newspapers), and then the sermons for the year were re-issued as a book at the end of the year. The first six volumes, from 1855-1860, are known as *The Park Street Pulpit*, while the next fifty-seven volumes, from 1861-1917 (his sermons continued to be published long after his death), are known as *The Metropolitan Tabernacle Pulpit*. He also oversaw a monthly magazine-type publication called *The Sword and the Trowel*, and Spurgeon wrote many books, including *Lectures to My Students, All of Grace, Around the Wicket Gate, Advice for Seekers, John Ploughman's Talks, The Soul Winner, Words of Counsel for Christian Workers, Cheque Book of the Bank of Faith, Morning and Evening*, his autobiography, and more, including some commentaries, such as his twenty-year study on the Psalms – *The Treasury of David*.

Charles Spurgeon often preached ten times a week, preaching to an estimated ten million people during his lifetime. He usually preached from only one page of notes, and often from just an outline. He read about six books each week. During his lifetime, he had read *The Pilgrim's Progress* through more than one hundred times. When he died, his personal library consisted of more than 12,000 books. However, the Bible always remained the most important book to him.

Spurgeon was able to do what he did in the power of God's Holy Spirit because he followed his own advice – he met with God every morning before meeting with others, and he continued in communion with God throughout the day.

Charles Spurgeon suffered from gout, rheumatism, and some depression, among other health problems. He often went to Menton, France, to recuperate and rest. He preached his final sermon at the Metropolitan Tabernacle on June 7, 1891, and died in France on January 31, 1892, at the age of fifty-seven. He was buried in Norwood Cemetery in London.

Charles Haddon Spurgeon lived a life devoted to God. His sermons and writings continue to influence Christians all over the world.

OTHER SIMILAR TITLES

WORDS OF WARNING,
BY CHARLES H. SPURGEON

This book, *Words of Warning*, is an analysis of people and the gospel of Christ. Under inspiration of the Holy Spirit, Charles H. Spurgeon sheds light on the many ways people may refuse to come to Christ, but he also shines a brilliant light on how we can be saved. Unsaved or wavering individuals will be convicted, and if they allow it, they will be led to Christ. Sincere Christians will be happy and blessed as they consider the great salvation with which they have been saved.

Available where books are sold.

JESUS CAME TO SAVE SINNERS,
BY CHARLES H. SPURGEON

This is a heart-level conversation with you, the reader. Every excuse, reason, and roadblock for not coming to Christ is examined and duly dealt with. If you think you may be too bad, or if perhaps you really are bad and you sin either openly or behind closed doors, you will discover that life in Christ is for you too. You can reject the message of salvation by faith, or you can choose to live a life of sin after professing faith in Christ, but you cannot change the truth as it is, either for yourself or for others. As such, it behooves you and your family to embrace truth, claim it for your own, and be genuinely set free for now and eternity. Come and embrace this free gift of God, and live a victorious life for Him.

Available where books are sold.

ACCORDING TO PROMISE,
BY CHARLES H. SPURGEON

The first part of this book is meant to be a sieve to separate the chaff from the wheat. Use it on your own soul. It may be the most profitable and beneficial work you have ever done. He who looked into his accounts and found that his business was losing money was saved from bankruptcy.

The second part of this book examines God's promises to His children. The promises of God not only exceed all precedent, but they also exceed all imitation. No one has been able to compete with God in the language of liberality. The promises of God are as much above all other promises as the heavens are above the earth.

Available where books are sold.

LIFE IN CHRIST (VOL. 1),
BY CHARLES H. SPURGEON

Men who were led by the hand or groped their way along the wall to reach Jesus were touched by his finger and went home without a guide, rejoicing that Jesus Christ had opened their eyes. Jesus is still able to perform such miracles. And, with the power of the Holy Spirit, his Word will be expounded and we'll watch for the signs to follow, expecting to see them at once. Why shouldn't those who read this be blessed with the light of heaven? This is my heart's inmost desire.

– Charles H. Spurgeon

Available where books are sold.

HONEST FAITH, BY CHARLES H. SPURGEON

The paragraphs of this little book are not supposed to be an argument. It was not my aim to convince an opponent but to assist a friend. How I have personally threaded the labyrinth of life thus far may be of helpful interest to some other soul who is in a maze. I hope that these pages will assist some true heart to say "he fought his doubts and gather'd strength." Let no man's heart fail him, for the prevalent skepticisms of today are but "spectres of the mind." Face them, and they fly.

Available where books are sold.

FOLLOWING CHRIST, BY CHARLES H. SPURGEON

You cannot have Christ if you will not serve Him. If you take Christ, you must take Him in all His qualities. You must not simply take Him as a Friend, but you must also take Him as your Master. If you are to become His disciple, you must also become His servant. God-forbid that anyone fights against that truth. It is certainly one of our greatest delights on earth to serve our Lord, and this is to be our joyful vocation even in heaven itself: *His servants shall serve Him: and they shall see His face* (Revelation 22:3-4).

Available where books are sold.

www.ingramcontent.com/pod-product-compliance
Lightning Source LLC
Chambersburg PA
CBHW070655130626
46553CB00005B/1718